The United States of Europe:
The Evolution of European Unity, 1918-2001

Table of Contents

Appendices
A.   Chronology
B.   Glossary
C.   "Declaration of Union"
D.   "The Tragedy of Europe"
E.   Map of European Union

Introduction

The concept of a unified Europe has been around for centuries. The Roman Empire, Charlemagne, the Mongols, Napoleon, and Hitler all attempted to unify Europe through military means, with various degrees of success, and all eventually failed. However, in the 20th century a new concept was attempted: to unify Europe through democratic means.

This paper will examine the growth of the European integration movement throughout the 20th century. It will discuss various influences on the movement, including the changing political fortunes across both the continent and the United States. It will consider the impact of national security issues and of domestic and international economies. It will examine the force of leadership personalities like Churchill and de Gaulle, as well as the strength and weakness of ruling coalitions. And, most significantly, it will highlight the essential link between economic prosperity and progress towards unification.

The European integration movement first took shape following the devastation of the First World War. Inspired first by the tenets of President Woodrow Wilson's Fourteen Points, Count Richard Coudenhove-Kalergi emerged as the most prominent advocate of European integration of the early 20th century. Through Coudenhove-Kalergi's efforts, French Premier Aristide Briand first broached the subject of a United States of Europe to the League of Nations. But the desperation of the Great Depression and the rise of Hitler in Germany led Europe to the Second World War and caused the European integration movement to find shelter in America.

During the post-World War II period, Winston Churchill emerged as the symbolic figurehead for unification. Finding strong support from Presidents Truman and Eisenhower, the movement found a leader in Jean Monnet, the most influential integration figure of the Cold War era. Intellectuals sought to find answers to the challenges of unification with concepts like functionalism and neo-functionalism. Under Monnet's guidance, the first step towards unification of the continent was realized with the groundbreaking formation of the European Coal and Steel Community (ECSC). The ECSC, followed soon by the European Economic Community (EEC), would provide the blueprint for unification efforts throughout the 20th century.

The promise of the 1960's was articulated in John F. Kennedy's "Grand Design," which sought a true economic partnership between Europe and the United States. In England, the political battle raged over a desire to join the EEC and a fierce determination to protect national sovereignty. In short order, however, the idealist hopes of the young American president and the English will to join the EEC ran counter to the political power and personality of French President Charles de Gaulle. His determination to reestablish the glory of France while also resisting American hegemony on the continent led to crisis in the EEC and a roadblock towards additional union.

De Gaulle's retirement from political life opened the door for expansion of the EEC, but the turmoil caused by the 1970's oil crisis and economic stagnation across Europe posed the next threat to integration. The general sense of malaise resulted in the rise of "Europessimism" which spread across the continent. Although a thaw in Cold War occurred when détente was achieved between the United States and the Soviet Union, political instability across Europe further undermined progress towards unification. By the mid-1980's, however, economic prosperity and the resumption of world leadership by the United States contributed to the signing of the Single European Act, which revitalized the movement as the end of the 20th century approached.

The 1990's brought the movement towards political integration to its greatest accomplishment, the Maastricht Treaty. Maastricht heralded the birth of the European Union (EU), which was the culmination of ninety years of effort towards political and economic integration on the European continent. The resulting organization fostered a financial juggernaut that challenged the United States for dominance of the global markets. But with this great achievement, the failure of the EU to effectively deal with international crises in Bosnia and Kosovo showed that Europe was still highly dependent upon the political and military leadership of the United States and the NATO alliance.

As the new millenium dawns, the continent stands on the verge of what Coudenhove-Kalergi and Monnet had longed dreamed: a European Union. Whether integration takes the final step of becoming a true European federal state or remains a union of independent nations remains to be seen.

I.   <u>Prelude: 1918-1939</u>

The First World War ended on November 11, 1918, after 4 years, 3 months, and 14 days. The aggregate direct war costs to all the belligerents amounted to approximately $186 billion. Some 37 million lives were lost as a direct result of the war, while another 10 million died through disease and starvation. By all accounts it was the costliest, bloodiest war in history to that date.

Besides the obvious destruction, the structure of Europe, which had been in place for centuries, was forever altered. Gone were the Austria-Hungarian Empire of the Habsburgs, the seven-century old Ottoman Empire, Imperial Germany, and Czarist Russia. A new world leader, President Woodrow Wilson of the United States, became the dominant figure of the peace negotiations. A country not yet 150 years old set the agenda for nations that were centuries old and began a journey that one day may lead to an integrated Europe.

President Wilson had been reluctant to enter the First World War, but once engaged he took a strong leadership role. Aware that Allied leaders were primarily concerned with national interests, Wilson pursued a more idealistic course. He developed his own plan for ending the war, known as the Fourteen Points.[1] The plan called for, among other things, freedom of the seas, weapons reductions, territorial adjustments between nations, self-determination, and, most importantly, the establishment of a League of Nations.

Using his points as the basis for a peace initiative, Wilson decided to personally lead the U.S. delegation during the peace negotiations. This was unprecedented; never before had a president left

---

[1] Wilson's Fourteen Points were designed to establish the basis for a just and lasting peace following the victory of the Allies in World War I and were contained in the president's address to a joint session of the U.S. Congress on January 8, 1918. The idealism expressed in the address was widely acclaimed and gave Wilson a position of moral leadership among the Allied leaders.

the United States while in office. Although Wilson's decision was bold, in the end it proved quite

costly because he was absent from the capital during the intense congressional debate to follow. [2]

In Europe, Wilson was received as a conquering hero. Viewed by many as a man of destiny,

he was the preeminent political leader in the world at that moment and a symbol of the New World

come to rescue the Old World. Unfortunately, many Old World leaders did not wish to be rescued.

English Prime Minister David Lloyd George and French Premier Georges Clemenceau considered

Wilson arrogant and unrealistic and worked to undermine his influence. Although aware of the

doubts other Allied leaders held for the Fourteen Points, public reaction persuaded Wilson that

popular opinion was overwhelmingly in his favor. Just as America's entry into the war had made a

major contribution to Allied victory, Wilson was now determined that American ideals would play a

major role the peace negotiations.

Wilson at first insisted that the Paris Peace Conference accept the full program laid out in the

Fourteen Points. However, Lloyd George and Clemenceau used Wilson's zeal for the all-important

fourteenth point, the League of Nations, as a bargaining chip. To win their support for the League,

the two European leaders forced Wilson to back down on many of the other points. As a result, the

Treaty of Versailles was considerably watered down from Wilson's original plan and the

disarmament, military occupation, and steep reparations forced on the defeated Germans returned to

haunt the Allies.

Wilson's absence away from home then came to a head. The midterm elections of 1918

resulted in the Republican Party gaining control of both houses of Congress. Under the leadership of

Senator Henry Cabot Lodge, who was both Majority Leader and Chairman of the Foreign Affairs

Committee, the Senate debated the treaty. Strong opposition emerged to some of the treaty's

provisions, most significantly that of collective security of League members. As the U.S.

---

[2] "Wilson, (Thomas) Woodrow," *Encarta 98 Encyclopedia*, CD-ROM (Seattle, WA: Microsoft Corporation, 1993-1997),

Constitution provides the Congress with sole power to declare war, a treaty that committed America to war without specific Congressional action was unacceptable. Despite intensive lobbying by the president, on November 19, 1919, the U.S. Senate rejected the Treaty of Versailles. The U.S. later signed a separate peace treaty with Germany, which formally ended the war for America.

Woodrow Wilson's prestige was severely damaged; in less than a year, he had fallen from the heights of world leadership to a mere politician. Unable to win the support of his own congress for a treaty he himself had designed and negotiated, his reputation on the continent was greatly diminished. While his grandest dream, the establishment of a League of Nations, was indeed achieved, the United States never became a member. In September of 1919 Wilson suffered a debilitating stroke and served out his presidency a broken man.

> After the future had vanquished the past on the battlefields of Europe, this past now took its revenge by defeating the future at the peace table…Shortly after the Fourteen Points had been killed in Paris, the League of Nations, as a world-embracing institution, was killed in Washington. The American isolationists completed the work of the European nationalists.[3]

Despite some failure with his initiatives and the disdain held for him by European politicians, President Wilson had a lasting influence on many other Europeans. A new generation emerged that was prepared to challenge conventional methods of relationships between nations on the continent. One such man was Count Richard Coudenhove-Kalergi, the most prominent advocate of European integration of the early 20th century.

Coudenhove-Kalergi was born in Japan to an Austrian government official in 1894. That he would prove to be the most persistent advocate of European unity prior to World War II is fitting, considering his family heritage of Dutch, Greek, German, Italian, Japanese, Norwegian, and Polish blood. He was raised in Austria and was there at the conclusion of the First World War, where he

---

accessed 20-24 December 2001.
[3] Richard N. Coudenhove-Kalergi, *Crusade for Pan-Europe* (New York: G. P. Putnam's Sons, 1943), 6.

followed the peace negotiations closely. Like many young Europeans after the Great War, he was deeply distrustful of old guard political leaders like Lloyd George and Clemenceau and came to admire the idealistic leadership offered by the American president. Despite the failure of the Fourteen Points, Coudenhove-Kalergi became an ardent Wilsonian.

Although largely forgotten today, Coudenhove-Kalergi became a leading advocate of European unification and was extremely influential during the inter-war years. In 1922, he founded the Pan-Europe Union, which favored the establishment of a single, supranational European state. Although it accomplished little on a practical level, the Pan-Europe Union was a prestigious organization. It counted among its members a number of esteemed European figures, such as Leon Blum and Aristide Briand in France, Winston Churchill, George Bernard Shaw, and Albert Einstein. In America, his supporters included former President Herbert Hoover, Senator J. William Fulbright, Allen and John Foster Dulles, and Claire Booth Luce.

As the European integration movement began to take shape, two competing philosophical strategies emerged: federalism and confederacy. Advocates of a federation, like Coudenhove-Kalergi, sought a true union of states to form a supranational Europe, along the lines of the United States of America. A strong central government required member nations to surrender a significant degree of sovereignty, an issue that was, and remains, a serious point of contention among countries that otherwise favored union (England, for example). The alternate path was the formation of a confederacy, a loose association of member states into an intergovernmental union with a weak central government and no loss of national sovereignty. These competing strategies dominated debates in the integration movement throughout the 20th century.

Coudenhove-Kalergi advocated the federalist approach. He greatly admired the work of Alexander Hamilton and believed that a United States of Europe should be based upon Hamilton's political philosophy.[4] However, being politically astute, he recognized that there was a natural resistance to federalism among nationalist forces throughout Europe and therefore moved deliberately. He preferred to work behind the scenes and was able to establish relationships with key government officials in both France and Germany.

The central issues that dominated post-World War I Europe were security and economics. In France, the issue was security; German armies had invaded five times in the past hundred years (1814, 1815, 1870, 1914, and 1918) and fear of the Prussian war machine was widespread. The war had bled France white and her population was only a third of Germany's. With Russia in the midst of civil war, Great Britain focused on her empire, and the United States pulled back within its own borders, France's World War I allies were not there to provide reassurance. As a result of these concerns, any meaningful movement to European integration had to address collective security.

In Germany, however, security was of little concern to the Weimar Republic; their first priority was economic recovery. The Treaty of Versailles had levied what Germany regarded as oppressive reparation payments on the German people, which stifled the economy. The loss of territory carried with it the threat of overpopulation and corresponding unemployment. With few natural resources and the loss of the Ruhr, Germany's principle industrial region, the government had to import most of its basic needs. In order to pay for those imports, it had to export what little agriculture it produced. With imports far outstretching exports, the nation was on the edge of economic collapse.

In Coudenhove-Kalergi's view, the solution to both the security and economic problems lay in the Pan-Europe movement. A period during which the Germany military was underdeveloped, he argued, was precisely the time to move towards a European federation, one that provided for the

---

[4] Ibid., 251-252. Hamilton is known as one of the principal authors of *The Federalist* papers and for his advocacy of a strong central government. Coudenhove-Kalergi's admiration for Hamilton ran deep: "The two greatest achievements humanity owes to America are federalism and aviation. The names of Alexander Hamilton and of Orville Wright have become symbols of creative leadership in politics and technology."

mutual defense of the continent that France desperately desired. Additionally, the reduction of protectionist tariffs and the development of a European market would allow both countries to pool resources and address Germany's crushing economic problems.

By November of 1928, national committees for Pan-Europe had been established throughout Europe. However, the Great Depression created a worldwide economic crisis that threatened to undermine Coudenhove-Kalergi's work. The limitations he faced became apparent: as a private, non-governmental organization, the Pan-Europe Union was powerless to achieve change. Essential to success was the ability to win the support of key government officials who could affect change. Coudenhove-Kalergi found his man in Aristide Briand.

In 1928, Briand was French foreign minister. He had long been an admirer of the Pan-Europe movement and was one of the key figures Coudenhove-Kalergi sought to influence for European union. In 1926, Briand had shared the Nobel Peace Prize with German Foreign Minister Gustav Stresemann for the Treaties of Locarno, a series of agreements designed to promote the security of western Europe. The two statesmen shared a common view of post-war Europe, that the fundamental key to peace was the relationship between France and Germany. They had worked hard to develop a rapprochement between their countries since the end of the First World War, which earned them the Nobel Prize.

In June 1929, Briand privately broached the subject of European integration to a meeting of the Council of the League of Nations, consisting of the foreign ministers of each member state. With Stresemann's vocal support, the other foreign ministers gave their approval of the plan. In July, Briand publicly announced his intention to recommend the establishment of a European union at the next Assembly of the League, scheduled for September. His announcement sent shock waves across Europe.[5]

---

[5] Coudenhove-Kalergi, *Crusade for Pan-Europe*, 129-130.

Briand was not at all sure how the announcement would be received in France. There were nationalists who saw the plan as unrealistic and a threat to national security. Others were suspicious that Briand was supporting a plan whose leading advocate, Coudenhove-Kalergi, was an Austrian. However, Briand's popularity had increased to such a degree that he was elected Prime Minister while retaining his portfolio as minister of foreign affairs. Sufficiently emboldened, Briand included the following passage on Pan-Europe in his inaugural address:

> For four years the ambitious program suggested by the phrase "United States of Europe" has been in my thoughts without my being able to commit myself to the gigantic task. However, after a painstaking examination of the whole question I have come to the conclusion that Europe will never be pacified as long as certain problems remain unsolved, certain suspicions unallayed, and as long as the nations of Europe do not try to find ways and means of collaboration.[6]

This speech was a watershed event for the movement. For the first time, the chief executive of a major European power had advocated the concept of integration. A Pan-European order was no longer merely the dream of an individual such as Coudenhove-Kalergi.

As promised, Briand took his case to the Assembly of the League of Nations on 4 September 1929:

> But I am convinced that some kind of union is necessary for nations who represent a geographic unit. Such nations should at least be able to associate in order to discuss their common interests, make common decisions and prove their solidarity in times of stress and tension. True, the union which we plan to bring about will have to deal with urgent economic problems...However, the union should prove advantageous also from a political and social point of view and it should do so without endangering any nation's sovereign rights.[7]

---

[6] Ibid.
[7] Ibid., 131-133.

Gustav Stresemann addressed the League Assembly on 8 September and placed his considerable prestige behind the concept.[8] He stated forcefully that he was prepared to consider any plan that resulted in a better-organized Europe and that Germany would cooperate with such a Europe.[9]

The League of Nations speech proved to be the zenith of Briand's dream and the fall from that high point was precipitous. Within days of his return to Berlin, Stresemann died unexpectedly; with him died Briand's initiative. Stresemann had been foreign minister for over six years and had guided German foreign policy through one of its most critical periods - he was simply irreplaceable. "For Briand, Stresemann's death was a disaster. He and Stresemann had been the two pillars that had supported the hopes of the new Europe. It was doubtful that Briand could bear the whole burden alone."[10] In Coudenhove-Kalergi's view, even the death of Briand would have been a lesser tragedy.

On May 17, 1930, Briand published his *Memorandum on European Union* and once member-nations had to respond formally to the initiative, support began to wane. At the second Pan-European Congress held in Berlin, Great Britain announced that she considered a European federation the only means of assuring peace and prosperity for the continent, and the government supported Briand's initiative. England, however, could not join such a federation because Britain's future was tied to its worldwide empire, not to Europe. Furthermore, the King's Government would never surrender sovereignty to a European state. Even Winston Churchill, in loyal opposition and an advocate of the movement, supported the government's position.[11]

Events in Germany ultimately decided the issue. Adolf Hitler's Nazi party made dramatic gains in the 1930 elections and became the second largest party in the Reichstag. President Paul von Hindenburg was, at age 83, an ineffectual leader and with Stresemann dead there was no

---

[8] Stresemann was a leader in stabilizing Germany in the inter-war years and provided respectability in the international community. He reoriented Germany's foreign relations toward reconciliation with the Allies and worked tirelessly to restore Germany to its former position of power.

[9] Ibid.

[10] Ibid.

[11] Ibid.

counterweight to the Nazi movement in Germany. Briand was defeated in a campaign for the French presidency in 1931 and died within a year. As Coudenhove-Kalergi stated, "The German elections defeated, in a definite manner, Briand and Pan-Europe."[12]

With the appointment of Hitler as German Chancellor in 1933, the "spirit of Locarno" was dead and events seemed to conspire for war. The Great Depression that started in America in 1929 and spread to Europe by the early 1930s, profoundly affected economies recovering from the First World War. In Italy, Benito Mussolini ordered the invasion of Ethiopia in 1935. The League of Nations did not respond, which severely damaged its credibility to effect peace. Germany withdrew from the League in 1933 and Italy in 1937. Great Britain and France each pursued a policy of appeasement towards Hitler and failed. By 1939, Europe was at war once again.

A period that began with such promise for meaningful change in Europe, based upon the idealism of Wilson's Fourteen Points, proved to be as illusory as the great economic prosperity of the 1920s. For Richard Coudenhove-Kalergi's Pan-Europe Union, there was a sense of opportunity lost. The fall of Austria caused him to relocate his movement to the United States. However, Coudenhove-Kalergi was well aware that the race that was the Pan-Europe movement was a marathon, not a sprint. As Europe descended into the abyss of war once again, he refocused the goals of his organization:

> The movement rejects the conception that Europe must unite at any price - even at the price of its culture and its freedom. It equally rejects extreme pacifism, which is prepared for the sake of peace to sacrifice that culture and that freedom. It prefers to postpone European union to a later date rather than to see it realised in the near future under the sway of a Bolshevist nationalist dictatorship...victory alone can ensure the creation of a United States of Europe. Britain, France, and their allies would dictate the terms of peace, and found the United States of Europe in order to make a third European war impossible, and create the foundations for European reconciliation and a common economic revival after the terrible waste of war...Such a union is often given the name 'the United States of Europe.' This name should signify no more

---

[12] Ibid.

than that the problem is one of unification of the states of Europe. It should in no way suggest an imitation of the United States of America, the political foundations of which are, and will remain, totally different from those of Europe.[13]

II.   Hot and Cold War: 1940-1961

Winston Churchill was perhaps the greatest wartime political leader in history. After assuming the office of prime minister in England's darkest hour, he led Great Britain from the virtual brink of defeat to overwhelming victory against Nazi Germany in the Second World War. Long a forceful advocate of European integration, as early as 1930 Churchill had written an article entitled, "The United States of Europe" for the *Saturday Evening Post*, which stated:

> The attitude of Great Britain towards European unification or "federal links" would, in the first instance, be determined by her dominant conception of a united British Empire. Every step that tends to make Europe more prosperous and more peaceful is conducive to British interests...We rejoice at every diminution of the internal tariffs and the martial armaments of Europe. We see nothing but good and hope in a richer, freer, more contented Europe commonalty. But we have our own dream and our own tasks. We are with Europe, but not of it.[14]

However, as the 1930s progressed Churchill became increasingly preoccupied with the threat from Nazi Germany. England and France declared war on Germany on September 3, 1939, and Churchill put aside the subject of European unity until he became prime minister on May 10, 1940.

By June of 1940, the war in France was going badly. German blitzkrieg had forced the French army into full retreat and the government of Prime Minister Paul Reynaud was near collapse. A group of Frenchmen, led by General Charles de Gaulle and economist Jean Monnet, presented to Churchill a plan for the establishment of a Franco-British Union. De Gaulle advised "some dramatic move was essential to give M. Reynaud the support which he needed to keep his government in the war, and suggested that a proclamation of the indissoluble union of the French and British peoples

---

[13] Richard N. Coudenhove-Kalergi, *Europe Must Unite* (Glarus, Switzerland: Paneuropa Editions Ltd., 1939), 139-153.
[14] Coudenhove-Kalergi, *Crusade for Pan-Europe*, 196.

would serve the purpose."[15] The Declaration of Union drafted by the British government declared that France and Great Britain would no longer be two nations but a single union. They would have common defense, foreign, and economic policies, joint citizenship, a single War Cabinet for the duration of the Second World War, and formal ties between the two parliaments. The British War Cabinet formally endorsed the proposal on June 16.[16]

De Gaulle recommended that Churchill travel to Paris to meet with Reynaud and the British prime minister was actually en route for the port of Southampton, where a ship was waiting to take him to France, when word came from Paris that the government had fallen. The will of the Reynaud government to resist had been broken and the French premier resigned rather than surrender, succeeded on June 16 by Marshal Henri Pétain. Instead of moving his cabinet to Africa to continue the war as Great Britain had hoped, Pétain agreed to an armistice with Germany on June 25, which gave the Nazis control of northern France and the Atlantic coast and established the French Vichy government in the unoccupied southeast. A momentous step towards European unification was therefore missed.[17]

When the Second World War ended in Europe on May 7, 1945, the result was a devastated and fragmented continent divided between an American Europe and a Soviet Europe. To many, an integrated Europe was the only way to regain control over their own future and to influence post-war world events. The next fifteen years saw an unprecedented emergence of various institutions and organizations dedicated to the growth of such a movement.

Throughout the war, Churchill periodically made statements regarding a post-war European union, but always in the most general terms. After 1945, when the Labor Party's electoral victory forced him to resign as prime minister, Churchill once again emerged as the most visible and vocal

---

[15] Winston S. Churchill, *The Second War World, Volume II: Their Finest Hour* (New York: Houghton Mifflin Company, 1940), 182.
[16] Ibid., 182-186. See Appendix C for complete text of "Declaration of Union."
[17] Ibid.

advocate for unification. At home and abroad, he employed his renowned rhetorical skills to develop support for the movement he viewed as the best means to heal the residual hatreds of World War II, prevent future wars, ensure economic prosperity, and allow Europe to compete with the superpowers.

Churchill was always a more vocal supporter of European union during his years out of power than he was during his two tours as prime minister. His proposal for the Franco-British Union was done at a time of extreme emergency, and in his memoirs Churchill is quick to note that it was more of a practical exigency rather than a long-sought goal.[18] The rhetoric of his public speeches, which suggested his strong support of a supranational state, was never equaled by his actions. At the heart of the issue was his oft-stated refusal to surrender Britain's sovereignty. The result was his quite vocal dedication to a movement that he would never agree to join. Upon his return to office, Churchill settled the issue quickly. On November 29, 1951, he announced that Britain should not become an "integral part of European integration" as it would "forfeit our insular or commonwealth wide character."[19]

Churchill's reticence in promoting Great Britain's membership in a European union should not overshadow his highly visible role as a leader of the movement, however. In Zurich on September 19, 1946, Churchill made his most famous unification speech, entitled "The Tragedy of Europe":

> Much work, Ladies and Gentlemen, has been done upon this task by the exertions of the Pan-European Union which owes so much to Count Coudenhove-Kalergi and which commanded the services of the famous French patriot and statesman Aristide Briand... I am now going to say something that will astonish you. The first step in the re-creation of the European Family must be a partnership between France and Germany. In this way only can France recover the moral and cultural leadership of Europe. There can be no revival of Europe without a spiritually great France and a spiritually great Germany. The

---

[18] Ibid., 180-181.

[19] Wendell Mauter, "Churchill and the Unification of Europe" in The Historian, 61(1), Fall 1998, pp. 67-84.

structure of the United States of Europe, if well and truly built, will be such as to make the material strength of a single state less important. Small nations will count as much as large ones and gain their honour by their contribution to the common cause. The ancient states and principalities of Germany, freely joined together for mutual convenience in a federal system, might take their individual places among the United States of Europe...Therefore I say to you: let Europe rise![20]

This dynamic speech, broadcast throughout Europe, had a profound effect on the movement. The prestige of Winston Churchill, no mere Utopian dreamer but a man who alone had stood up to Hitler and Mussolini in 1939, one of the "Big Three" Allied leaders, and a man considered by many the greatest practical politician of the century, brought previously unequaled attention to European unity.[21] The speech provided the spark activists like Richard Coudenhove-Kalergi had long sought. Grass-roots European union groups sprang up throughout the continent and formed a loose organization called the International Committee of the Movements for European Unity. The committee met at The Hague on May 7-10 1948, an event known as The Congress of Europe.

Over 800 people representing 24 European organizations attended the event, including observers from the United States and Great Britain. Churchill, the Congress's Honorary President, addressed the opening session on the afternoon of May 7. A rally was held on May 9, attended by some 40,000 people in support of European unity. The Congress concluded with a pledge of support for a United Europe and called for the establishment of a Charter of Human Rights, a Court of Justice, and a European Assembly.[22]

The Zurich speech also served as a catalyst for other pro-European movements. In 1949, an organization called the Council of Europe was established, designed to achieve a greater unity among the member nations. The ten original member nations include Belgium, Denmark, France,

---

[20] Winston S. Churchill, *Winston S. Churchill: His Complete Speeches 1897-1963*, ed. Robert Rhodes James, vol. 7 (New York: Chelsea House Publishers, 1974), 19 September 1946, 7379-82. See Appendix D for complete text.
[21] Richard N. Coudenhove-Kalergi, *An Idea Conquers the World* (London: Hutchinson & Co., Ltd., 1953), 268-269.
[22] Ibid., 286-290.

Great Britain, Ireland, Italy, Luxembourg, Netherlands, Norway, and Sweden. The council consisted of two main bodies: the Committee of Ministers and the Parliamentary Assembly.

The Committee of Ministers served as the decision-making body of the council and provided a forum for debate. As such, it was composed of the foreign ministers of the member states and met at least twice a year. The Parliamentary Assembly consisted of 239 representatives and an equal number of alternates, all chosen from the parliaments of the member nations. The assembly, which met four times a year, was responsible for making recommendations to the Committee of Ministers.

The Council of Europe served in a purely advisory capacity, with each member nation retaining full sovereignty. But it did serve as a useful forum in which urgent European and world issues could be debated. In working toward the goal of a united Europe, the council ultimately proved to be a predecessor to the European Union.

As the unification movement rumbled in the background, the United States took stock of the situation in Europe. Emerging from the war as a superpower, America abandoned her previous isolationist policies and adopted a number of new policies that indicated a long-term commitment to the continent. Harry Truman, who assumed the American presidency upon the death of Franklin Roosevelt in 1945, had initially hoped that the Soviet Union and the Anglo-American Allies could reach agreement on the status of eastern European countries, resulting in free elections. By early 1947, however, it was apparent that the Soviet Union was determined to consolidate control over its satellite states and pursue an aggressive policy against the West. Truman responded with a series of bold foreign policy steps that committed the U.S. to European security.

On March 13, 1947, in response to a crisis in Greece and Turkey, Truman made an address that proved to be the most controversial of his presidency. "I believe it must be the policy of the United States to support free peoples who are resisting attempted subjugation by armed minorities or by outside pressures."[23] His statement, which was the genesis of what became known as the Truman Doctrine, resulted in U.S. aid to anti-Communist forces in Greece and Turkey. The Truman Doctrine was later expanded to justify support for any nation that the United States government believed was threatened by Communism.

Truman's next initiative was the European Recovery Program. In June 1947, Secretary of State George C. Marshall outlined an offer of aid from the United States to assist in the economic restoration of post-war Europe. The Marshall Plan, as the program came to be known, provided financial aid to devastated European countries, prompted by fears of the spread of Communism while Europe was unable to defend itself.

The U.S. provided the money and goods, but the Europeans themselves had to develop a plan for using the aid effectively.   The European plan had to be a comprehensive joint effort, as opposed to individual national requests. In 1948, Austria, Belgium, Denmark, France, West Germany, Great Britain, Greece, Iceland, Italy, Luxembourg, the Netherlands, Norway, Sweden, Switzerland, Turkey, and the United States signed an accord that established the Organization for European Economic Cooperation (OEEC). Through the OEEC, the Marshall Plan ultimately invested over $13 billion into Europe and greatly contributed to the economic recovery of the continent.[24]

A new theoretical movement called *functionalism* emerged at the same time to provide justification for policies like the creation of the OEEC. Functionalist theories state that the "two basic and observable trends in modern history are the growth of technology and the spread and intensification of the desire for higher standards of material wealth." Functionalists believed that these two trends could provide the basis for peace. The classic example of functionalism was the railroads. The emergence of inexpensive and reliable transportation allowed for greater economic

---

[23] Ed Cray, *General of the Army: George C. Marshall, Soldier and Statesman* (New York: Cooper Square Press, 1990), 596.

growth and greater productivity. In order to exploit the railroad, governments had to agree on minimum international standards (i.e., track gauge, etc.). Increased production and trade as a result of railroads increased material wealth and acted as incentive for greater cooperation between nations.[25]

The most influential advocate of functionalism was David Mitrany, who argued in the 1940s that citizens would pressure their governments to increase international cooperation in order to take advantage of new technologies. Functionalists were not concerned with politics and nations, but with economics. Technology would inevitably lead to the growth of specialized skills. The development of "professional pride" in these specialties and a desire to continue innovation would result in the emergence of "functional" organizations that would cross over geographical and national borders. These international nongovernmental organizations (NGOs) promoted prosperity and cooperation by focusing initially on politically non-controversial goals. The NGOs would therefore not be limited by nationalist concerns over sovereignty and prestige and could therefore be a powerful tool towards peace.[26]

A variation to functionalism was then developed by the French economist Jean Monnet,[27] author of the Monnet Plan for French participation in the Marshall Plan and founder of the Action Committee for the United States of Europe (ACUSE) as a vehicle to promote closer European integration. A determined federalist, Monnet could not accept the functionalist conclusion that independent nations were irrelevant, but as an economist he recognized the value of some functionalist tenets. Monnet outlined a related doctrine called neo-functionalism, which emphasized

---

[24] The Marshall Plan achieved both its immediate and long-term aims. When the aid ended in 1952, Communist control of Western Europe had been averted, the region's industrial production stood 35 percent above prewar levels, and West Germany was independent, rearming, and economically booming.

[25] Harold K. Jacobson, *Networks of Interdependence* (New York: Alfred A. Knopf, 1979), 67.

[26] Ibid., 68-69.

[27] **Jean Monnet** (1888-1979), French statesman and financier. He served as first deputy secretary general of the League of Nations and was active in international financial affairs through the 1920s and '30s. After WW II he developed a plan for France's economic recovery. Served as first president of the European Coal and Steel

interstate economic cooperation and expanded it to include cooperation along political lines. Neo-functionalism led to the term *l'engrenage*, or "the expansive logic of sector integration." Monnet viewed *l'engrenage* as a method to engage interest groups and national officials in a partnership of both economic and political means.[28]

Monnet would prove to be a key figure in European unity. While Churchill had been the most visible advocate of integration, Monnet had become the most influential figure in the post-war period. Critical to his success were his vast political connections. Although never a politician himself, his influence through the 1950s and 1960s was widespread among key leaders throughout the world, including Churchill, French Foreign Minister Robert Schuman, Charles de Gaulle, John Foster Dulles, and George W. Ball.

As an economist, Monnet focused on a plan to provide economic incentives for cooperation. On May 9, 1950, French Foreign Minister Robert Schuman proposed the creation of a common authority to regulate the coal and steel production in West Germany and France. Under the Schuman Plan, which had been drafted by Monnet, membership was also open to other Western European countries. The plan was widely applauded and in 1951 Belgium, France, Italy, Luxembourg, the Netherlands, and West Germany (known as the Six) signed the Treaty of Paris creating the European Coal and Steel Community (ECSC).[29]

Although ostensibly designed to establish a coal and steel common market, the ECSC was actually much more. It provided the initial platform for the neo-functionalist theory of its founder, Jean Monnet. Member states envisioned that, "the pooling of coal and steel production

---

Community. In 1955, Monnet founded the Action Committee for a United States of Europe. Considered the "Father of Europe."

[28] Jacobson, *Networks of Interdependence*, 71-72.

[29] David Armstrong, *From Versailles to Maastricht: International Organisation in the Twentieth Century* (New York: St. Martin's Press, 1996), 143-144.

should…provide for…a first step in the federation of Europe."[30] Most importantly, the ECSC also

produced a hierarchy that served as the blueprint for future integration (see Table 1).

Once again reflecting Monnet's beliefs, the ECSC was established within a strong federalist

framework. During negotiations for the treaty, France had insisted that participation in the

negotiations required prior acceptance to a degree of supranationality and a corresponding reduction

of national sovereignty. Supranationality was a deliberate act by France to keep Britain out of the

ECSC, because France realized that England would not agree to any requirement to transfer

sovereignty to a central authority. As the French hoped, Great Britain decided not to join the

ECSC.[32]

The ECSC exceeded economic expectations. Between 1952 and 1960, Europe saw a 75%

increase in coal and steel production and a 58% increase in industrial production.[33] However, the

political gain was even more dramatic. Monnet, who served as first president of the ECSC (1952-

1955), viewed the executive structure as a critical step toward European economic and political

integration. By guaranteeing a source of income directly to the High Authority, the ECSC was

provided a degree of independence and therefore a first step towards federalism. Although it never

---

[30] Ibid., 144.

[31] *Europe Today: National Politics, European Integration, and European Security*, ed. Ronald Tiersky (Lanham, MA: Rowman & Littlefield, 1999), 451-454. Individual organizations identified in Glossary.

[32] Armstrong, *From Versailles to Maastricht*, 143-144.

[33] *Columbia Electronic Encyclopedia, Sixth Edition*, online edition, under "European Coal and Steel Community," accessed on *Earthlink*, 24 February 2002.

quite achieved the integration Monnet hoped (and therefore may have exposed some of the inherent flaws in neo-functionalism), the ECSC did result in a shift away from political and military confrontation toward cooperation and is to this day considered as the vital first step towards the European Union.[34]

Moving from narrow economic collaboration to broader political cooperation proved more problematic. Since the emergence of the Cold War, the U.S. had pressed for increased cooperation among European states, particularly in the area of defense. Security became even more critical with the outbreak of the Korean War, which was widely seen as an effort by the Soviet Union to divert American attention away from Communist expansion in Europe. In order to counter the perceived Soviet threat while American forces were otherwise engaged in Korea, the European Defense Community (EDC) was developed.

The EDC was proposed in 1950 by the French government as the Pleven Plan. The EDC was to operate as an army comprised of troops from France, Germany, Italy and the Benelux countries (Belgium, Luxembourg, and the Netherlands) and serve as a counterbalance the overwhelming conventional military strength of the USSR in Europe. To offset fears of German rearmament, the forces would be under European leadership. The goal of the Pleven Plan was to provide European security while reducing the need for large-scale U.S. forces in Europe.

After initial reservations regarding the relationship between the EDC and NATO, both the Truman and Eisenhower administrations strongly supported the EDC. Although the smaller members of NATO were keen, the Scandinavian countries were cool toward the idea, and opinion in France and Italy was divided. Where the ECSC's economic nature had widespread support across the continent, the EDC's focus on military defense was received with much more trepidation. European governments were prepared to surrender some degree of sovereignty over economic

---

[34] *Europe Today*, ed. Ronald Tiersky, 451-454.

issues, but national defense remained an area of great sensitivity. A treaty was actually concluded in Paris in 1952, but, as the Korean War ended and invasion by the Soviet Union began to seem less likely, the perception of necessity for the EDC also diminished. Although the French had initiated the plan, there remained a strong reluctance to allow German rearmament in any form. After forcing a series of delays, the French parliament ultimately killed the EDC when it failed to ratify the Treaty in August 1954.[35]

With the EDC dead, the Western European Union (WEU) was created in its place. It was established in Brussels in 1955 as a defensive, economic, social, and cultural organization, consisting of Belgium, France, Great Britain, Italy, Luxembourg, the Netherlands, and West Germany. With European defense provided by NATO and economic coordination by the European Economic Community, the primary function of the WEU was to supervise the rearmament of West Germany. Although it remains in existence to this day, the WEU never attained the promise that America hoped would be achieved by the EDC.[36]

From the late 1940s into the 1950s, no American was a stronger advocate of a unified Europe than Dwight Eisenhower. For over three years he had worked tirelessly to maintain the alliance while leading the Allied victory in Europe. Upon his assignment in 1950 as Supreme Commander of Europe (SACEUR) and of North Atlantic Treaty Organization (NATO) forces, he advocated a Germany that was rearmed, unified, and brought into NATO as a full partner.

In Eisenhower's view, a strong and unified Europe would be able to take a larger and more active role in their defense. In his role as SACEUR, he had been initially unimpressed with the EDC concept. Within six months, however, he changed his mind. The ability of NATO to provide only 14 or 15 divisions against the overwhelming conventional ground forces of the Soviet Union made the defense of Europe wholly dependent upon America's nuclear umbrella. Eisenhower realized the

---

[35] Ibid., 147-148.

key to a meaningful Allied conventional force was inclusion of West German forces, hence his new support for the EDC. "I am shifting my position…I am certain that there is going to be no real progress towards a greater unification of Europe except through the medium of specific programs of this kind [EDC]."[37]

The General's opinions carried great weight on the continent. On July 3, 1951, he addressed the English-Speaking Union in London before 1,200 British leaders. He was introduced as "the First Citizen of the Atlantic," "the man who won the war," and then Winston Churchill led a standing ovation for him. Eisenhower called for a United States of Europe: "With unity achieved, Europe could build adequate security and, at the same time, continue the march of human betterment that had characterized Western civilization." Although too deaf to hear the speech, Churchill read it the next day and told Eisenhower, "I am sure this is one of the greatest speeches delivered by any American in my lifetime."[38]

When Eisenhower assumed the presidency in 1952 he brought his advocacy of European unity to the White House. He wanted to move forward on the establishment of a United States of Europe, and he saw the EDC as the perfect vehicle for achieving his goals.[39] His support went beyond his concern for the continent, however. A stronger Europe, tied together economically and militarily and protected by the NATO nuclear umbrella, would increase security for the United States and allow the president to reduce the U.S. military budget. Eisenhower wrote, "EDC, in short, would simultaneously provide greater security for the West, a smaller defense establishment for the United States, and lower taxes."[40]

---

[36] Armstrong, *From Versailles to Maastricht*, 148.

[37] Stephen E. Ambrose, *Eisenhower: Soldier, General of the Army, President Elect, 1890-1952, Volume One* (New York: Simon and Schuster, 1983), 508.

[38] Ibid., 509.

[39] Ambrose, *Eisenhower: Soldier and President*, 334.

[40] Ibid.

A key figure in the Eisenhower administration was his secretary of state, John Foster Dulles. Dulles had impeccable credentials in foreign affairs. An expert in international law, he had participated in the negotiations of the Treaty of Versailles. Although a lifelong Republican, he had served as an advisor in foreign affairs to both the Roosevelt and Truman administrations. Widely known as a staunch anti-Communist, Dulles was also a long-standing advocate of European unity. He had become an advisor to Richard Coudenhove-Kalergi and attended the Congress of Europe in 1948. He was known as a strong supporter of the EDC by the time that he was tapped to head the State Department.

Eisenhower was determined to see the EDC succeed and placed a fair amount of his presidential prestige behind the movement. He sent his secretary of state to lobby personally European governments for their support and Dulles threatened an "agonizing reappraisal" of American foreign policy if the EDC was not approved.[41] When the French government failed to ratify the treaty in 1954, it was widely seen as a major foreign policy setback for the Eisenhower administration. The president himself considered it a major setback for European integration, and the event marked the dawn of an extended chilly relationship between the United States and France.

Ultimately, the French veto of the EDC resulted in what France feared most – an independent West Germany. As promised, immediately upon receiving word of the vote Eisenhower called for a meeting of the NATO countries, "with a view of including Germany as an equal partner therein."[42] West Germany became a member of NATO within a year.

In June 1955, the foreign ministers of the Six gathered once again to consider proposals for further economic integration. The resulting Treaty of Rome of March 1957 created the European Economic Community (EEC), which was based upon the structure introduced by the ECSC (see Table 1). The four branches were: the European Commission, with executive authority (formerly the

"High Authority"); the European Parliament, with legislative authority (formerly the "Common Assembly"); the European Court of Justice, with judicial authority (formerly the Court of Justice); and the Council of Ministers, again with a single representative from each member state to protect national sovereignty.

The EEC was the most significant of the original European communities. The treaty called for the gradual elimination of trade barriers between member nations, the development of a common tariff for imports from the rest of the world, and the creation of common policy for managing and supporting agriculture. The treaty provided for a greater role for national governments than had the ECSC treaty, but allowed for a larger supranational role as economic integration progressed. The resulting "common market" provided economic cohesion for the continent. The EEC provided the basis for the future European Union. [43]

Still wary of joining any organization that threatened the Crown's sovereignty, Great Britain once again chose not to join a European organization. In response to the economic challenges of the EEC, the European Free Trade Association (EFTA) was formed in 1960, where Austria, Denmark, Great Britain, Norway, Portugal, Sweden, and Switzerland established their own free trade bloc. Although it continued in a much scaled-down fashion through the end of the 20th century, the EFTA never quite equaled the influence or achieved the success of the EEC.

The post-war period in Europe was a dynamic time. European integration movements took shape under the leadership and influence of Churchill and Monnet. The Truman administration abandoned the prior American fondness for isolation and became firmly engaged in European affairs. The Eisenhower administration continued this trend and, by support for both the ECSC and the EDC, encouraged a greater degree of European unity. However, the promise of the 1950's soon

---

[41] Henry Kissinger, *The Troubled Partnership: A Re-Appraisal of the Atlantic Alliance* (New York: Published for the Council of Foreign Relations by McGraw-Hill, 1965), 33.

[42] Amborse, *Eisenhower: Soldier and President*, 372.

[43] *Europe Today*, ed. Ronald Tiersky, 452.

gave way to an escalation of the Cold War, a reduction of English influence on the continent, and change in France and West Germany which adversely impacted the integration movement and, at the same time, the relationship between the United States and Europe. We turn to these developments in the next section.

III.   The Grand Design: 1962-1969

Europe made considerable strides forward in the cause of integration during the 1950s. The period between 1962 and 1969, however, was marked by significant change on both sides of the Atlantic Ocean. In Europe, Charles de Gaulle became the dominant political figure in France while the British Commonwealth slowly dissolved. In the United States, John F. Kennedy succeeded Dwight Eisenhower and introduced a new generation of leadership. The relationship between de Gaulle and Kennedy (and between de Gaulle and Kennedy's successor, Lyndon Johnson) played a critical role in the movement towards European integration.

In 1961 the Kennedy administration took office and pursued an activist policy regarding Europe. Not since the presidency of Woodrow Wilson was foreign policy so infused with a sense of idealism. After winning the Democratic presidential nomination, Kennedy established a Foreign Policy Task Force to develop foreign policy proposals for use during the campaign. The key figure of the task force was George W. Ball. Ball, who served as Undersecretary of State for Economic Affairs in the Kennedy administration, was another of Jean Monnet's many disciples and something of a protégé.[44] He headed the State Department group known as the "Europeanists," and proved to be remarkably influential in both the Kennedy and Johnson administrations. Ball recognized that while America was still the preeminent economic power, it no longer dominated the world economy as it had since the end of World War II. The Marshall Plan had proven to be remarkably successful and the European economy was growing at twice the rate of America's. Consequently, the U.S. faced challenges to both its economic and political leadership for the first time in a generation.

In the Task Force report, Ball proposed the concept of a "partnership Between a United Europe and America within a Strong Atlantic Community."[45] The United States should form a partnership with a united, supranational Europe. With no single figure (like the American president) or single body (like the American Congress) in Europe to negotiate with, a meaningful increase in trade across the Atlantic was difficult to achieve. "When one partner possesses over 50 percent of the resources of an enterprise and the balance is distributed among sixteen or seventeen others, the relationship is unlikely to work very well." In Ball's view, real partnership was only possible among equals.[46]

Jean Monnet had long advocated the "twin pillars" or "dumbbell" argument. As former Secretary of State for Eisenhower, Christian Herter wrote at the time, "I believe the present [Kennedy] Administration…holds the…view, which has come to be termed the "dumbbell" concept – meaning that an economic and political alliance is stronger if it has been agreed to by partners of equal weight on both sides.[47] Ball's concept became the genesis of the administration's European foreign policy. In a speech presented on July 4, 1962, Kennedy outlined the basis for what came to be known as the "Grand Design." The plan called for a "concrete Atlantic partnership," between a united Europe and the United States.

The Grand Design was viewed with suspicion in France. Charles de Gaulle had been elected president of the French Fifth Republic in 1958. The Treaties of Rome had been signed prior to his assumption of office, but he was supportive of the EEC. Although he did not approve of the

---

[44] *John F. Kennedy and Europe*, eds. Douglas Brinkley and Richard T. Griffiths (Baton Rouge, LA: Louisiana State University Press, 1999), 265-266.
[45] Ibid., 272.
[46] Henry Kissinger, *The Troubled Partnership: A Re-Appraisal of the Atlantic Alliance* (New York: Published for the Council of Foreign Relations by McGraw-Hill, 1965), 236.
[47] Ibid., 236-237.

supranational aspect to the treaties, the requirement for unanimous vote provided France (and all members) with a veto of any action of which they did not approve, effectively protecting their sovereignty. De Gaulle viewed the veto as a powerful weapon and one essential for French participation. In addition, the EEC provided the means for de Gaulle to increase French political power on the continent, provide framework for a Franco-German rapprochement, and promote France's economic and agricultural advancement.

In America, de Gaulle was widely viewed as an obstructionist. Presidents' Eisenhower, Kennedy, and Johnson all had their share of difficulties dealing with the French leader regarding European affairs. De Gaulle was, however, an effective advocate of European integration for the purpose of enhancing French power, although along strictly confederate lines. An intense nationalist, he was determined to ensure France's independence and restore her former glory. Because he viewed the United State's influence on the continent to border on hegemony, he often challenged American power. European integration therefore allowed de Gaulle to achieve two goals: to provide France a platform to remain a major power, and to provide a counterweight to U.S. power.

The supranational concepts proposed under the Grand Design were simply unacceptable to de Gaulle. Henry Kissinger framed the argument in this manner: "Where United States spokesmen stress the concept of partnership, de Gaulle tends to emphasize the idea of equilibrium."[48] This effectively captures the essence of the issue: a European confederation, of which an independent France was both a member and a leader, was acceptable; a supranational United States of Europe was not.

De Gaulle advocated a return to the "Big Three" mentality of the Second World War, as the President of the French National Assembly stated:

---

[48] Ibid., 46-47.

> The most complete coordination should exist between the three Western Powers that have responsibilities extending beyond their borders. These are the United States, which is the leader and the greatest power of the West; the United Kingdom, which has special ties with the Commonwealth; and France...General de Gaulle is working for a united Europe and is in constant touch with West Germany and the other nations of Europe. This makes France the natural channel for the coordination of policies on the continent in the same way in which the United States and the United Kingdom are the natural channels for the coordination of policies in other geographical areas.[49]

De Gaulle saw Europe as the natural "backyard" of France, and was determined to defend her prerogatives on the continent. His views account for de Gaulle's efforts to keep Great Britain out of the EEC (which, given Britain's reluctance to surrender any degree of sovereignty, was not hard to do) as well his reasons for pulling out of the NATO military structure.

In 1961, de Gaulle proposed a French plan for European union to the EEC. Called the Fouchet Plan, for the French ambassador to Denmark who actually announced the proposal, the plan was a thinly veiled attempt to dilute the Community's supranational bent. Claiming the EEC lacked authority and political effectiveness, the plan sought to amend the Treaties of Rome to provide for a "Union of States." This proposed union would establish common defense and foreign policies and increased cooperation in other areas, such as science and education, but remain intergovernmental.[50]

West German leader Konrad Adenauer pledged West Germany's support for the plan. The remaining members of the Six, however, were less enthusiastic. The move towards an intergovernmental system conflicted with the supranational framework of the treaties. De Gaulle's insistence that all decisions require unanimous agreement only blocked future EEC political growth.

---

[49] *John F. Kennedy and Europe*, eds. Douglas Brinkley and Richard T. Griffiths (Baton Rouge, LA: Louisiana State University Press, 1999), 322.

[50] Intergovernmentalism: This term is used to refer to the mechanisms and procedures that have been established in order to facilitate governments working together and cooperating on certain fields while simultaneously retaining their sovereignty. This approach to integration works in opposition to federalism, aiming at keeping supranational institutions to a minimum. The European Free Trade Association and The Organization for Economic Cooperation and Development are examples of organizations that are essentially intergovernmental. Intergovernmentalism is generally

Finally, and perhaps of most concern to the smaller states, the establishment of a defense policy outside of NATO angered both the United States and Great Britain. As a result, the smaller Benelux countries opposed the treaty. Much as de Gaulle feared American domination of Europe, these smaller countries feared an eventual Franco/German domination. Finally, the removal of the supranational framework was unacceptable to a majority of the Six.

The Dutch insisted on British participation, aware that de Gaulle would not agree to British membership. Because de Gaulle preferred to see the plan fail rather than see it diluted, negotiation was hopeless and political agreement of the Six was impossible. In April 1962, negotiations over the plan collapsed and the concept died. De Gaulle's response to the failure of the Fouchet Plan was to be expected. At a press conference in May, he stated, "…only the states are valid, legitimate and capable of achievement…At the present there is and can be no Europe other than a Europe of States – except, of course, a Europe of myths, fiction, and pageants."[51]

De Gaulle sought an opportunity to respond to the failure of the Fouchet Plan. Determined to reinforce his view that England have no direct political role in Europe, he found the perfect vehicle to clearly establish his point: the proposed expansion of the European Economic Community. Great Britain struggled economically and politically during the latter half of the 1950s. Economic growth rates were considerably lower than the Six and the EFTA proved to be a poor substitute for the EEC. The Suez Crisis[52] had seriously undermined British prestige and marked the first split between the US and the UK. Although still opposed to any surrender of national independence, British business and political leaders concluded that European Community membership was in the UK's best interest.

---

considered attractive by those who espouse national sovereignty and nationalism over supranationalism. (From the *EU Dictionary*)

[51] Alessandro Silj, *Europe's Political Puzzle: A Study of the Fouchet Negotiations and the 1963 Veto* (Cambridge, Mass: 1967). Silj provides a comprehensive discussion of the events surrounding the Fouchet Plan.

[52] **Suez Crisis**: In July 1956, French, Israeli, and British forces invaded Egypt to take back the Suez Canal, which Egyptian leader Gamal Abdel Nasser had nationalized. President Eisenhower refused to support the move and forced the invaders to withdraw. As a result, the government of Prime Minister Anthony Eden fell and British prestige was further diminished.

In August of 1961, Denmark, Ireland, and the United Kingdom applied for EEC membership; Norway applied the following April.

Belgium, Germany, Italy, Luxembourg, and the Netherlands indicated support for expansion and the Kennedy administration endorsed the move as well. De Gaulle, however, immediately sent veiled signals that he was opposed to British membership. He feared that the United Kingdom's membership would provide a challenge to French leadership. He was also suspicious of the Grand Design, and viewed Kennedy's endorsement of the English application as merely a means to install an American proxy within the EEC. "If Britain came in, de Gaulle had said, the Common Market would have to admit a lot more countries; and in that case 'a colossal Atlantic community would emerge under American dependence and control, which would soon swallow up the European Community.'"[53]

De Gaulle was determined that this would not happen. In a famous press conference on January 14, 1963 de Gaulle announced that he could not support British membership in the EEC. He stated Britain might, "one day come round to transforming itself enough to belong to the European Community without restriction and without reservation, placing it ahead of anything else…[but] England is not yet prepared to do this."[54] Unwilling to join without the United Kingdom, Denmark, Ireland, and Norway withdrew their applications shortly after.[55]

The veto of British membership in the EEC was a serious blow to the government of Prime Minister Harold Macmillan. The original decision not to join the community had been controversial

---

[53] Nora Beloff, *The General Says No: Britain's Exclusion from Europe* (Middlesex, England: Penguin Books, Ltd., 1963), 15.

[54] *John F. Kennedy and Europe*, eds. Douglas Brinkley and Richard T. Griffiths (Baton Rouge, LA: Louisiana State University Press, 1999), 330.

[55] Never one to forget a slight, de Gaulle's antipathy towards the United States went back to the summer of 1943, when the Roosevelt administration supported General Henri Giraud as leader of the French National Committee over de Gaulle. The French president never acknowledged that he owed his eventual rise to head of the Free French forces to Churchill's strong support and Roosevelt's reluctant acceptance. Throughout the Second World War, de Gaulle's housing, his income, and his support staff were all funded directly from the British government. Although he owed his political life to the fact that Churchill had stood up to Roosevelt, he repaid his debt by claiming the British "could always be relied upon to take the American side." See Beloff, *The General Says No*, 33-37.

in Europe; the decision to apply now had been controversial at home. The British government had lobbied hard for membership and de Gaulle's veto caused Macmillan great embarrassment and further undermined British influence on the continent. The French action also angered the other members of the Six. The decision itself was no surprise, as de Gaulle's position was well established. However, the rest of the EEC did not appreciate the manner in which he announced his decision – at a press conference, while formal negotiations were still being conducted.

De Gaulle continued to pursue French independence from foreign influence, even that of his partners among the Six. In 1965 the Commission president offered two major proposals for consideration. The first suggested that the EEC raise its own revenue directly, as opposed to receiving contributions from member states. The second recommended implementing majority voting in place of unanimous voting.

De Gaulle quickly responded to the proposals. He felt that the establishment of direct taxation was the responsibility of a sovereign nation, not of the Community. Additionally, majority in place of unanimous voting significantly increased the authority of the Commission and the European Parliament, with a corresponding decrease in authority of the Council of Ministers. De Gaulle argued that this showed the Treaties of Rome to be ambiguous or flawed, and refused to consider the proposals. When the remaining members of the Six continued to push for negotiation of the proposals, de Gaulle responded by directing all French representatives on the Council of Ministers to boycott meetings and withdrew his representative from EEC headquarters in Brussels. This protest became known as the "Empty Chair Crisis," which effectively halted Community operations for six months.[56]

The crisis ended in January 1966 with the Luxembourg Compromise, which essentially accepted the French position. The Six agreed that when issues of great significance were to be

---

[56] Ibid.

decided, the Council of Ministers would try to reach unanimity. De Gaulle chose to interpret this to mean they must reach unanimity. The other members pointed out that the treaty specifically called for the use of majority voting unless otherwise stipulated in the treaties, but otherwise let the matter drop. The proposals that had caused the crisis were quietly removed from consideration and the EEC went back to business as usual.

The Luxembourg Compromise may be seen as less of an agreement as an "agreement to disagree." A Pandora's box could potentially result from the compromise; any member state could hold up an issue by simply declaring it a "very important national interest" and insisting on unanimity. The practical results of the compromise was that, in order to avoid this occurrence, the Council in the future deferred an issue unless a unanimously acceptable solution could be found, regardless of whether the treaties prescribed majority voting.[57]

The United States' relationship with France under President de Gaulle continued to suffer. His determination to ensure France's independence in defense matters was particularly acute following the Suez Crisis. Eisenhower's decision not to support the action in Egypt was considered by de Gaulle as a betrayal. Furthermore, his perception that Great Britain abandoned France at the first sign of U.S. disapproval was further proof that France could depend only on herself. The Suez Crisis, which had divided England and caused the Eden government to fall, conversely served to unite France and strengthen her independent action.[58]

To de Gaulle, an independent French military meant pursuit of an independent nuclear capability. Launched in the early 1950s, the program met significant American resistance for two principle reasons. First, the Eisenhower administration had a general policy against the proliferation of nuclear weapons. Second, reinforcing concerns about proliferation, was a widespread belief that

[57] Ibid.
[58] *John F. Kennedy and Europe*, eds. Douglas Brinkley and Richard T. Griffiths (Baton Rouge, LA: Louisiana State University Press, 1999), 36.

the French government was deeply penetrated by Communists.[59] Despite American resistance de Gaulle continued; Soviet entry into the nuclear club in 1949, West German admission to NATO in 1955, and the Suez Crisis of 1956 each provided additional incentive.

In 1959, de Gaulle withdrew the French navy from NATO; he kept most of his army out of NATO control as well. In order to address the French nuclear concerns, late in the 1950s the U.S. introduced a program called the multilateral force (MLF). The MLF called for the creation of a surface fleet armed with Polaris missiles and under the control of NATO. Similar in many ways to the European Defense Community of the mid-1950s, the MLF would provide Germany with the means to participate in European defense. Lingering concerns regarding a rearmed Germany would be addressed by providing each NATO member with a veto over the use of nuclear weapons.[60]

Although the MLF was intended to placate France, de Gaulle strongly objected. Since actual control of the nuclear warheads remained with the United States, he saw the MLF merely as an attempt by the U.S. to retain superiority and to keep France out of the nuclear club. Despite lukewarm support from some members of the Kennedy administration (most notably from George Ball at State and General Lauris Norstad, SACEUR), MLF never won much support. Secretary of Defense Robert McNamara was one of the program's chief opponents. The plan continued until finally cancelled by President Johnson in 1965.[61]

Once de Gaulle was reelected in 1965, an independent French defense policy continued. Although he at times stood shoulder-to-shoulder with the United States (most notably during the Cuban Missile Crisis), his arrogant demeanor and sense of pride continued to symbolize the distant relationship between France and America. In 1967, he achieved his goal of removing all French forces from the NATO military command. That same year he also vetoed Great Britain's second

---

[59] Ibid.
[60] Ibid., 42.
[61] Ibid., 52-55. Chapter 4, "The MLF Debate," provides a detailed review of the program within the Kennedy administration and in Europe.

application for EEC membership, making it clear that any expansion of the European Community had to wait until he was out of power. He resigned the presidency following defeat in a national referendum in April 1969 and retired.

With the death of John Kennedy in November 1963, Lyndon Johnson assumed the presidency. He retained the Kennedy cabinet and continued most of his predecessor's policies. While the Soviet Union remained the focal point of America's foreign policy (as it had with every president since Truman), Johnson did not embrace the Grand Design and many events emerged to draw his attention away from the continent. The president developed a strong personal enmity for de Gaulle and America's relationship with France continued to be strained. The Arab-Israeli Six-Day War in June 1967 and the invasion of Czechoslovakia by the Soviet Union in August of 1965 were particular challenges. The primary focus of Johnson's attention was, of course, the Vietnam War. As U.S. involvement escalated, criticism of the war in America reached unprecedented heights. Although he received nominal support from his European allies, the war in Southeast Asia undercut Johnson's role as a world leader.

The situation in Europe changed upon de Gaulle's retirement. Georges Pompidou, the new French president, in general continued most of his predecessor's policies. However, momentum was gathering for expansion of the European Community. The rest of the Six were clearly in favor of growth and began to view France as obstructionist. With the dynamic presence of Charles de Gaulle removed from the equation, France's position was untenable.

Political relationship on the continent began to shift. West Germany saw the rise of Social Democrats like Willy Brandt, who embraced a more activist style of leadership. Brandt's policy of *"Ostpolitik"*[62] signaled a shift away from the dependence on France that had marked the Adenauer government. Although he personally shared de Gaulle's suspicions about Great Britain's true loyalties, Pompidou worried about the growing independence of West Germany and he began to see England as a potential ally once again. Coupled with the more Euro-centric leadership of Edward Heath in Great Britain, the French president was willing to consider expansion. In 1969 at the Hague Summit, Pompidou supported membership for Denmark, Ireland, and Great Britain. Additional plans were debated to increase integration, including the pursuit of a single currency. Following lengthy and sometimes difficult negotiations, the United Kingdom, Ireland and Denmark joined on the European Community January 1, 1973.[63]

All of the obstacles to European unity cannot be laid solely at de Gaulle's feet, however. The European Defense Community had failed four years before he had even assumed office. While de Gaulle remains to many today as the very epitome of the arrogance and inflexibility of France, a federal union of Europe still does not exist on the continent thirty years after his death.

Henry Kissinger wrote about the American role regarding European integration:

> Our strong support of supranational, federal institutions has contributed to the stalemate in European discussions. While not sufficient to bring about our preferred solution, our influence is strong enough to block approaches with which we disagree. Moreover, despite our ardent support for European unity, our impact has often been the contrary of what was intended. While affirming the need for European integration, we have unintentionally tended to undermine a European sense of identity.[64]

IV.   Détente and Decay: 1970-1991

Beginning in the 1970s, the two principle elements of European unity, the economy and the political situation of the several nations, experienced significant change. The fifteen years following EEC expansion was marked by serious economic recession, which affected the entire western world.

---

[62] *Ostpolitik*, German for "eastern policy," called for initial reconciliation between the two Germanys. See A. W. DePorte, *Europe Between the Superpowers: The Enduring Balance* (New Haven: Yale University Press, 1979), 185-186.
[63] David Armstrong, *From Versailles to Maastricht: International Organisation in the Twentieth Century* (New York: St. Martin's Press, 1996), 166-170.
[64] Henry Kissinger, *The Troubled Partnership: A Re-Appraisal of the Atlantic Alliance* (New York: Published for the Council of Foreign Relations by McGraw-Hill, 1965), 240.

Politically, the relationships between France, Great Britain, the United States, and West Germany experienced fundamental change. Each country produced one dominant leader who served relatively long terms in office: Ronald Reagan in the U.S. (8 years); Margaret Thatcher in Great Britain (11 years); François Mitterrand in France (15 years); and Helmut Kohl in Germany (18 years)(see Table 2). Additionally, there was a significant change in the superpower relationship with the advent of détente. Although the harsh rhetoric of the Cold War clearly decreased, economic malaise and the shifting leadership resulted in limited progress towards European union.

United States	United Kingdom	France	Germany
Nixon, 1969-1974	Wilson, 1964-1970	Pompidou, 1969-1974	Brandt, 1969-1974
Ford, 1974-1976	Heath, 1970-1974	Giscard, 1974-1984	Schmidt, 1974-1982
Carter, 1976-1980	Wilson, 1974-1976	Mitterrand, 1981-1995	Kohl, 1982-1998
Reagan, 1980-1988	Callaghan, 1976-1979		
Bush, 1988-1992	Thatcher, 1979-1990		
	Major, 1990-1997		

Table 2 - National Leaders of the Major Atlantic Powers, 1970-1991

In France, President Valéry Giscard d'Estaing continued the conservative policies of de Gaulle and Pompidou. He was a strong proponent of the European Community and expanded France's relationship with Third World nations. France had long worked to establish closer relations with the Soviet Union as well, and as détente improved Cold War tensions it also helped to thaw Franco-U.S. relations. Giscard has less success at home, where his efforts to address the economy largely failed, and industrial growth fell for the first time since the end of the war. In 1976, Giscard introduced a wide-ranging program of economic reforms in an attempt to revitalize France's recession-bound economy. Despite his efforts, the effects of the economic malaise were acutely felt in France and he was defeated in the 1981 elections.

François Mitterrand, the first Socialist president of France, replaced Giscard in 1981. Mitterrand served as French president for nearly 15 years, longer than any other person. He initially employed classic socialist methods to improve the economy: nationalize banks and major industries, including chemicals, electronics, and steel; decentralize government by giving more powers to local and regional offices; and enact social reforms such as an increased minimum wage. By 1982, rising inflation and unemployment caused Mitterrand to reverse many of his policies and adopt a more conservative, free-market approach.

In West Germany, Willy Brandt continued to employ his activist program to moderate success. He reversed Konrad Adenauer's isolationist policy regarding East Germany and for his efforts was awarded the 1971 Nobel Peace Prize.[65] He was replaced by fellow-Social Democrat Helmut Schmidt in 1974, who continued to reinforce both Atlantic and European relations. Throughout the 1970s, inflation and rising unemployment undercut the West German economy. High profile terrorist activities, such as the death of 11 Israeli athletes during the 1972 Summer Olympic Games in Berlin and a wave of attacks by groups such as Baader-Meinhof, contributed to a high level of domestic instability. In 1982, Christian Democrat Helmut Kohl became the new chancellor of West Germany.

Kohl assumed office at a propitious time. By the mid-1980s, West Germany was joining the ranks of the U.S. and Japan as one of the world's leading economic powers. As domestic conditions improved, West Germany expanded its leadership in the Community and in international affairs. Furthermore, Kohl was a child during the Second World War and the first postwar German leader not to have a Nazi taint. He led Germany for longer than any man in the post-war period, first as chancellor of West Germany (1982-1990) and then as chancellor of the reunited Germany (1990-1998).

In Britain, the period was marked by instability of the national government, which resulted in a corresponding reduction of leadership and influence on the continent. From 1970 to 1991, Great Britain had six prime ministers. Harold Wilson (Labor) had succeeded Harold Macmillan and led Britain through the latter half of the 1960s. Wilson was followed by Edward Heath (Conservative), whose major accomplishment was overseeing Great Britain's admission into the European Community. In 1974, the Conservative government fell and Heath returned for his second tour as PM. The economy continued to suffer, with inflation peaking at over 25% and unrest spreading in Northern Ireland. Heath suddenly retired in 1976 and was succeeded by James Callaghan (Conservative). Callaghan attempted to manage a severely troubled economy and growing labor unrest with a slender parliamentary majority.

In 1979, Margaret Thatcher (Conservative) became the first woman to serve as prime minister of Great Britain. She was elected on a promise to reverse Britain's economic decline by reducing the role of government and reintroducing greater latitude for the free market. Her approach resembled the campaign slogan of Ronald Reagan, with whom she developed a close friendship. Thatcher won reelection in 1983 and 1987 and became the only British prime minister in the 20th century to serve three consecutive terms. There was a wide swing in economic conditions during her administration, but her resistance to commit Great Britain to full economic integration in the Community ultimately contributed to her resignation. Thatcher was succeeded by John Major (Conservative), who became party leader and prime minister in 1990.

There were common economic and political trends among the principle European leaders of the post-war era. For the most part, each led countries experiencing severe economic turmoil. In addition, several also faced a near evenly divided Parliament, resulting in narrow majorities. Divided electorates in turn, significantly limited their ability to govern independently with a long-

---

[65] A. W. DePorte, *Europe Between the Superpowers: The Enduring Balance* (New Haven: Yale University Press, 1979),

term view. Combined with the pressures of the Cold War, these common threads provided a degree of political instability in Western Europe.

Across the Atlantic, the United States retained its position as leader of the Free World despite political upheaval associated with the Vietnam era. Richard Nixon made dramatic advances in foreign affairs by ending the war in Vietnam, achieving détente with Communist leaders, and personally travelling to the Soviet Union and Communist China. However, the domestic scandal of Watergate resulted in his resignation in disgrace from office in 1974. Gerald Ford served the remainder of Nixon's term, but his pardon of Nixon and dire economic conditions resulted in Jimmy Carter's election in 1976. Carter served only a single term, undone by overwhelming economic issues and the Iranian hostage crisis.

In 1980, Ronald Reagan was elected president. Conservative leadership, significant economic revival, military build-up, and a reestablishment of the U.S. as the dominant power marked Reagan's two terms in office. American prestige, both economically and militarily, increased greatly throughout the world under Reagan's leadership. He was succeeded by his vice president, George Bush, whose significant accomplishments in foreign affairs (The Gulf War, reunification of Germany, and the collapse of the Soviet Union) were offset by domestic economic woes.[66]

The economic miracles of the post-war period ground to a halt in the 1970s as the Community's first enlargement coincided with the economic downturn. The Yom Kippur War in October 1973 had a worldwide impact. Combined with the decision by the Organization of

185-186.

[66] It is interesting to note that only three presidents served two complete terms in office during the second half of the 20th century: Dwight Eisenhower, Ronald Reagan, and Bill Clinton. While constant leadership change had negative impact on many European nations (particularly Great Britain), the underlying strength of the American economy and of its political system allowed her to retain her preeminent role throughout the post-World War II and post-Cold War periods.

Petroleum Exporting Countries (OPEC)[67] to raise prices, western economies were rocked. The resulting oil crisis sparked rampant inflation, rising unemployment and deficit spending throughout Europe.

Among the European Community as a group, their payments surplus of $11 billion in 1973 became a deficit of $22 billion in 1974. Initial attempts to establish European Community energy policies failed and various members pursued bilateral agreements with individual OPEC countries. Some "experts" even predicted the crisis might cause a major shift in international relations, with the energy-poor Europeans realigning with the oil-rich Middle East, at the expense of U.S.-European relations.[68]

Such dire predictions did not come true, of course, but the impact on individual national economies was near catastrophic and amounted to the most significant threat to the industrial world since the Great Depression. From the mid-1970s to the mid-1980s the EU stagnated and went from one budgetary crisis to another. The sense of a general malaise growing from economic stagnation resulted in the coining of a new word: "Europessimism."[69] This term came to represent the feeling across the continent that the economy had bottomed out and government was incapable of redressing the situation. The political and economic conditions created a veritable Catch-22: weak political leadership fed poor economic conditions, and poor economic conditions resulted in instability in the government and the election of weak leaders with no clear mandate. These conditions inevitably served to weaken the commitment of European governments towards the integration movement.

---

[67] **OPEC**: The Organization of Petroleum Exporting Countries, an international organization primarily concerned with coordinating the crude-oil policies of its member states. Founded in 1960, the 12 members meet to regulate oil prices worldwide and establish production ceilings.

[68] A.W. DePorte, *Europe Between the Superpowers: The Enduring Balance* (New Haven: Yale University Press, 1979), 208.

[69] David Armstrong, *From Versailles to Maastricht: International Organisation in the Twentieth Century* (New York: St. Martin's Press, 1996), 165. See Chapter 7, "The European Union, 1970-1985: Turbulence, Europessimism, and Eurosclerosis," 165-187.

The full impact of the Luxembourg Compromise of 1966 was now felt. While the common markets created by the European Community were clearly a success, the political union that people like Jean Monnet felt would inevitably follow was not realized. Although the concept of majority voting remained as part of the Treaties of Rome, the implied requirement for unanimity of the compromise remained in effect. As long as this standard remained in place, there could no real movement toward a more formal union. As a result, there was a sense on the continent that the EEC might not be the panacea advocates such as Monnet had hoped.

A second factor that contributed to the limited movement towards unification was the establishment of the European Council during the European Community Summit in Paris in 1974. The Council was added to the existing structure of the EEC (see Table 1) and was comprised of the Heads of Government of each member of the Community. This arrangement served to provide another level of intergovernmentalism, which was once again in conflict with the supranational framework of the Treaties of Rome.[70]

An unmistakable fact emerged at this time: European integration was tied to economic prosperity. When conditions were good, the open markets contributed to prosperity for all ECC members. When conditions worsened, countries turned inward and were resistant to surrendering national control to any supranational body. This fact can be seen throughout the 20th century, when boom times (the 1920's, 1950's, and 1990's) produced the most significant movement towards European union.

Despite conditions on the continent, the machinery of the European Community ground on. In 1976, the Tindemans Report on European Union was published. The report called for common foreign and defense policies, a common monetary plan, and increased social and industrial policies. It also called for the establishment of an organization along federal lines, with a supranational

---

[70] Ibid., 176.

executive branch independent of national governments and accountable to an elected, bicameral parliament. Although the Tindemans Report was clearly too radical for many members to accept at that time, the European Union later embraced many of its concepts.[71]

From the early 1980s, economic conditions began to improve and the paralysis that had affected the EEC was lifted. There was consensus on the continent that the system needed an injection of political will. As a result, the Single European Act (SEA) was enacted in 1986. It provided a framework for a single European market and for closer cooperation in the science and environmental areas. While the SEA provided little substantive change to the Treaties of Rome, it was significant because it was the first formal amendments to the treaties and it addressed the ambiguities that President de Gaulle had manipulated so skillfully in the 1960s. Ultimately the SEA proved to be the necessary next step on the road to union.

The momentum that was gained by the enactment of the SEA received a monumental push forward with the fall of the Berlin Wall on November 9, 1989. October 1990 brought the reunification of Germany, soon followed by the formal dissolution of the Soviet Union on December 31, 1991. In the vacuum created by the fall of communism, the structure and economic stability of the European Community provided a valuable base. The potential concerns of Europe over Germany reunification was offset by the EEC immediately admitting East Germany into the Community (actually, by recognizing the significantly increased German market) and allowing those markets to be accessed.

In 1991, the European Community members met to deliberate the next step. Debate broke out once again on which form the next step towards integration would take, although couched in new terms. One side favored the "tree with branches" model, along federal lines. The competing

---

[71] Ibid., 176.

strategy was the "three pillars" approach, which guaranteed intergovernmentalism. Once again, there remained a strong commitment to sovereignty and the pillars approach was adopted.[72]

The Treaty of European Union (TEU) was signed at Maastricht, Netherlands, on February 7, 1992.[73] Widely known as the Maastricht Treaty, the treaty provided the second major amendments to the Treaties of Rome. Maastricht provided for a single currency by 1999, a common foreign and security policy and co-operation on justice and home affairs. In addition, the treaty also changed the formal title of the European Economic Community to the European Union and the tenets were based on the "three pillars:"

> Pillar One: Incorporated the existing EEC treaties as well as the SEA, establishes Union citizenship, Community policies, and set out the institutional requirements for the European Monetary Union (EMU);
> Pillar Two: established the Common Foreign and Security Policy, which makes it possible for the Union to take joint action in foreign and security affairs (remains intergovernmental);
> Pillar Three: created the Justice and Home Affairs (JHA) policy, which refers to police and judicial cooperation in criminal matters (also remains intergovernmental).[74]

The reunification of Germany created a state with over 80 million citizens and 30% of the gross national product of the EEC, creating a Goliath with the potential to overwhelm France and Great Britain in economic might. In a gesture of leadership intended to calm any latent fears of a reunified Germany, Chancellor Helmut Kohl became the leading advocate of the treaty. France, in an act consistent with her post-war philosophy, also supported the TEU in order to contain German strength and reduce American hegemony in Europe.[75]

The TEU, clearly Europe's most ambitious treaty to date, faced a difficult ratification process. All twelve members had to approve it before the EU could be put into place. In rapid

---

[72] Ibid., 200-201.

[73] The TEU was ratified by the 12 members of the European Community: Belgium, Denmark, France, Germany, Great Britain, Greece, Ireland, Italy, Luxembourg, the Netherlands, Portugal, and Spain. In 1994 the EU admitted three more members: Austria, Finland, and Sweden.

[74] Ibid., 200-201.

[75] Henry Kissinger, *Does America Need a Foreign Policy?* (New York: Simon & Schuster, 2001), 47.

fashion, the Danish electorate rejected the treaty by a small majority and the French electorate barely passed it, 51%-49%. A resulting monetary crisis delayed plans for a single currency. After negotiating a series of "opt-outs"[76] to safeguard Danish concerns, the Netherlands approved the treaty by a wide margin in the second referendum and the twelfth member formerly signed the TEU.

The struggle to win approval of the Maastricht Treaty convinced European leaders that the electorates were uneasy about the speed of EU change. There were clear inadequacies in the TEU, which had to be addressed before integration could continue. However, it was clear across the European continent and the world that the establishment of the European Union was the most significant post-World War II event regarding union.[77]

The twenty-year period that began in 1970 was not very promising for the European union movement. Economic dishevels, political instability, and a general sense of malaise covered the continent. With the 1980s, however, came a robust world economy and movement within the European Community towards developing the structure for future change. The Single Europe Act provided the first spark; it was followed it rapid succession by the fall of the Berlin Wall, reunification of Germany, and dissolution of the Soviet Union. Further change came in the post-Cold War era.

V.   Post-Cold War and Beyond: 1993-2001

The dissolution of the Soviet Union, and with it the end of the Cold War, was clearly the most significant event of the second half of the 20th century. George H. W. Bush was president of the United States during this tumultuous period. With an extensive background in foreign affairs, including U.S. ambassador to the UN from 1971-1973 and eight years as vice president, Bush proved to be the most active president in foreign affairs since Richard Nixon. He was supportive of

---

[76] **Opt-out**: This is a facility for member states that choose not to participate in a particular activity of the Union, which

German reunification and of the establishment of the European Union. Maastricht marked a new era in European relations both within the continent and across the world. The Atlantic Alliance was still clearly in place, but the relationship between America and Europe was a matter of debate as the Clinton administration took office.

President Clinton initially focused on addressing the domestic economic issues and sent signals that America might pull back from its European commitments to a limited degree. However, he proved to be willing to provide military force in Europe in support of humanitarian intervention. Following the example set by the Bush administration's decision to send forces to Somalia, Clinton embraced a humanitarian role for his administration, particularly in support of United Nations resolutions. Under the banner of both the UN and NATO, President Clinton provided military forces in support of humanitarian operations in Haiti and in the Balkans. The Dayton Peace Accords of 1995 ended the largest use of NATO forces in the alliance's history and was followed by the insertion of U.S. ground troops in Bosnia to enforce the peace. The leadership role played by the Clinton administration in Bosnia and later Kosovo proved two things: first, that the U.S. was committed to remaining engaged in European affairs, and secondly that despite the economic success of the EU, Europe was still incapable of acting forcefully as an integrated political bloc.[78]

For the foreseeable future, it is apparent that NATO will remain the primary European security system. The Clinton administration also made clear that the United States will not abandon the former Soviet Bloc nations, but rather pursue economic and, perhaps, military ties as well. This commitment is seen in plans to expand NATO, set to occur roughly in parallel with expansion of the European Union. The dual enlargement of both NATO and the EU is no historical coincidence; European security and European integration remain intertwined more than ever before. "The United

---

may be part of a Treaty. It is usually agreed during the negotiations of the Treaty and appears as a protocol to it.
[77] *Europe Today*, ed. Ronald Tiersky, 269.
[78] Kissinger, *Does America Need a Foreign Policy?*, 264-272.

States has too much at stake in Europe, beginning with trade, and too much history and culture in common with the European peoples, including Russia, to permit a retreat into isolationism."[79]

The U.S. and Great Britain continue to enjoy a "special relationship" and our strongest ally continues to be a key aspect to U.S. policy in Europe. The British view of America remains, for the most part, fundamentally unchanged. While France always casts a suspicious eye on America, England has viewed the U.S. as a partner (albeit, a very much senior partner) since the end of World War II (or even, as Kissinger argued, since the end of World War I). As the British government navigates its path into the 21st century, it is dedicated to European Union membership while still maintaining sovereignty. As such, the relationship with the United States remains the central theme to British foreign policy. [80]

France remains, as always, wary of American hegemony. However, despite the French government's occasionally chilly political relationship with the U.S. over the issue of hegemony, in every significant crisis of the Cold War period – the Berlin Crises, the Cuban Missile Crisis, and the Gulf War – France has proven to be a staunch ally. However, as Foreign Minister Hubert Vedrine stated in a speech in November 1999, France continues to pursue a policy to reduce American dominance over the continent:

> American supremacy today is…felt in the economy, in monetary affairs, in technology and in military fields, as well as in lifestyles, language and the mass culture products that are swamping the world, shaping ways of thinking, and exercising a fascination that even works on adversaries of the United States…In keeping with America's view both of itself and the rest of the world over the last two centuries, most great American leaders and thinkers have never doubted for an instant that the United States was chosen by providence as the "indispensable nation" and that it must remain dominant for the sake of humankind…Americans have no doubts and the more forthright amongst them are quick to remind us that the contemporary world is the direct outcome of Europe's complete failure to manage its own and the world's affairs in the first half of the twentieth century.[81]

---

[79] *Europe Today*, ed. Ronald Tiersky, 11-12.
[80] Ibid., 49-51.
[81] Kissinger, *Does America Need a Foreign Policy?*, 48-49.

With regards to the United States, Germany's position remains somewhere in the middle between Britain and France. The German government remains a dedicated NATO ally and to this day houses thousands of American troops on her territory. The U.S. role in the post-World War II recovery of a unified German state is fully recognized and appreciated. Committed to the European Union, the single largest power still struggles to define a legitimate role on the continent. For this reason, leaders both inside Germany and in the other European nations continue to recognize the need for American leadership as insurance against aggression both within and without Europe.[82]

The European Union also faces a bright if uncertain future. The supranational goals of Richard Coudenhove-Kalergi and Jean Monnet have still not been reached, although there has been monumental growth towards that goal. The Treaty Of Maastricht, while a flawed document, has set the course for integration for at least the next couple of decades. In October 1997, the Foreign Ministers of the fifteen member countries of the EU signed the Treaty of Amsterdam. Continuing the incremental approach towards integration, the treaty does not replace but rather amends the Treaties of Rome and Maastricht. Although it still falls far short of taking the next step towards a federal state, it does reconcile some imbalances of the TEU. The new treaty established new policies in four areas: freedom, security and justice; citizenship of the Union; common foreign policy; and reform of EU institutions.[83]

The EU has proved to be a popular club in the post-Cold War era. By the close of the 1990s, more than a dozen countries had applied for membership[84] with only three being accepted: Austria, Finland, and Sweden. Norway had applied and been accepted on two occasions but the action has failed to receive a majority vote in national referendums. In 1991, the EU joined with the European

---

[82] Ibid., 50-52.

[83] *Europe Today*, ed. Ronald Tiersky, 271.

[84] EU Applicants: Turkey (1987), Cyprus (1990), Malta (1990), Switzerland (1992), Hungary (1994), Poland (1994), Romania (1995), Slovakia (1995), Latvia (1995), Estonia (1995), Lithuania (1995), Bulgaria (1995), and the Czech

Free Trade Association to establish the European Economic Area (EEA). The EEA, which took effect on January 1, 1994, established a single market for goods and eliminated trade barriers between the EU and EFTA, each of which is the other's largest trading partner.[85]

The next significant event under the Treaty of Maastricht was the establishment of a single European currency. In March 1979, the European Monetary System (EMS) was established as a first step towards achieving an Economic and Monetary Union (EMU). The EMS was intended to stabilize exchange rates and curb inflation, and required member governments to effect economic policies to prevent deviation from the central rate. The practical result was the need to coordinate domestic economic policy. During the 1980s, the EMS was able to achieve lower inflation rates throughout the EU and ease the impact of global currency fluctuations.[86]

The EMU was formalized under the Treaty of Maastricht and designated a zone of countries within the EU that share common monetary policy and currency: the euro. Effective January 1, 1999, the euro was the approved single European currency, managed under the independent European Central Bank. On January 1, 2002, the euro was placed into circulation. The treaty provided a transition period during which the use of the euro will not be obligatory. By January 2002, twelve of the fifteen EU member countries[87] had agreed to participate in the common currency.

The establishment of the European Union was the culmination of over ninety year's work to integrate the European continent. As the 20th century proved, integration always found its strongest ally in economic prosperity. Through the rubble of two world wars, economic prosperity and crisis, and a debilitating cold war, the dream of people such as Richard Coudenhove-Kalergi and Jean

---

Republic (1996). Of these countries, six – Bulgaria, Czech Republic, Hungary, Poland, Romania, and Slovakia – are considered associate members of the EU.

[85] *Europe Today*, ed. Ronald Tiersky, 234-236.

[86] Ibid., 453.

[87] EMU participating members: Austria, Belgium, Finland, France, Germany, Greece, Ireland, Italy, Luxembourg, the Netherlands, Portugal, and Spain. Great Britain, Denmark, and Sweden opt out of participation.

Monnet has persevered. Although debate still remains over the final path integration will achieve – supranationality or intergovernmentalism – there is a blue print for the future based upon the Treaties of Rome and Maastricht.

During the same period, the United States has provided support for the integration movement in Europe. Abandoning isolationist tendencies of the first half of the 20th century, America has remained dedicated to the Atlantic Alliance's goals of peace and prosperity. Henry Kissinger has stated, "the emergence of a unified Europe is one of the most revolutionary events of our time."[88] Throughout the evolution of an integrated Europe, the U.S. has provided material aid, economic prosperity, military security, and political support. At times, it seemed that integration continued only because it was urged onto reluctant allies.

Whether the European Union ever actually becomes a United States of Europe is still in doubt. French President Jacques Chirac has offered a popular and clever observation, stating that the EU is, "aiming not for a United States of Europe but for a United Europe of States."[89] Only time will tell what path Europe eventually follows, but what seems clear is that the fundamental relationship between Europe and America, based even today upon the tenets of the Atlantic Charter, remains a strong and crucial Atlantic Alliance.

---

[88] Kissinger, *Does America Need a Foreign Policy?*, 47.

[89] "Reading Room: Visions of EU," *Time.com*, URL: <http://time.com/time/reports/visions/ash3.html>, accessed 9 March 2002.

Bibliography

Ambrose, Stephen E. *Eisenhower: Soldier, General of the Army, President Elect, 1890-1952, Volume One.* New York: Simon and Schuster, 1983.

_____. *Eisenhower: Soldier and President.* New York: Simon and Schuster, 1990.

Armstrong, David, and others. *From Versailles to Maastricht: International Organisation in the Twentieth Century.* New York: St. Martin's Press, 1996.

Barnett, Richard J. *The Alliance: America, Europe, Japan, Makers of the Postwar World.* New York: Simon and Schuster, 1983.

Beloff, Nora. *The General Says No: Britain's Exclusion from Europe.* Middlesex, England: Penguin Books, Ltd., 1963.

Churchill, Winston S. *Winston S. Churchill: His Complete Speeches 1897-1963.* Ed. Robert Rhodes James, vol. 7. New York: Chelsea House Publishers, 1974.

_____. *The Second War World, Vol II: Their Finest Hour.* New York: Houghton Mifflin Company, 1940.

Columbia Electronic Encyclopedia, Sixth Edition. Online edition. Under "European Coal and Steel Community." Accessed on *Earthlink*, 24 February 2002.

Coudenhove-Kalergi, Richard N. *An Idea Conquers the World.* London: Hutchinson & Co., Ltd., 1953.

_____. *Crusade for Pan-Europe.* New York: G. P. Putnam's Sons, 1943.

_____. *Europe Must Unite.* Glarus, Switzerland: Paneuropa Editions Ltd., 1939.

Cray, Ed. *General of the Army: George C. Marshall, Soldier and Statesman.* New York: Cooper Square Press, 1990.

DePorte, A. W. *Europe Between the Superpowers: The Enduring Balance.* New Haven: Yale University Press, 1979.

Europe Today: National Politics, European Integration, and European Security. Ed. Ronald Tiersky. Lanham, MA: Rowman & Littlefield, 1999.

Jacobson, Harold K. *Networks of Interdependence.* New York: Alfred A. Knopf, 1979.

Kissinger, Henry. *The Troubled Partnership: A Re-Appraisal of the Atlantic Alliance.* New York: Published for the Council of Foreign Relations by McGraw-Hill, 1965

_____. *Does America Need a Foreign Policy?* New York: Simon & Schuster, 2001.

Mauter, Wendell. "Churchill and the Unification of Europe." *The Historian* 61, no. 1, Fall 1998.

"Reading Room: Visions of EU." *Time.com.* URL: <http://time.com/time/reports/visions/ash3.html>. Accessed 9 March 2002.

APPENDIX A

Chronology

1910-1919

Jan 8 1918   President Wilson presents "Fourteen Points" proposal to Congress.

Nov 11 1918   World War I ends.

Jun 28 1919   Treaty of Versailles signed.

Nov 19 1919   U.S. rejects Treaty of Versailles.

1920-1929

Nov 15 1920   League of Nations established.

4 Sep 1929   French Premier Aristide Briand makes "United States of Europe" speech at League of Nations.

1930-1939

Jan 1933   Adolf Hitler becomes Chancellor of Germany.

1940-1949

Jun 16 1940   Winston Churchill presents his "Declaration of Union" between France and Great Britain to British War Cabinet.

Aug 14 1941   Atlantic Charter signed.

May 8 1945   World War II ends in Europe.

Oct 24 1945   United Nations founded in San Francisco.

Sep 19 1946   Winston Churchill delivers his "Tragedy of Europe" speech.

Jun 5 1947   European Recovery Program (Marshall Plan) is announced.

Apr 1948   Organization for European Economic Cooperation (OEEC) is established.

May 7-10 1948   Congress of Europe meet in the Hague.

Apr 4 1949   North Atlantic Treaty signed.

May 1949   Council of Europe is formed.

1950-1959

May 9 1950   Schuman Plan is announced.

Apr 1951   Treaty of Paris signed, establishing the European Coal and Steel

Community (ECSC).

Aug 1954	French National Assembly rejects Treaty of Paris (European Defense Community treaty).
Mar 1957	Treaties of Rome are signed, establishing European Economic Community (EEC).

1960-1969

Jan 4 1960	The European Free Trade Association (EFTA) established.
Jul 4 1962	President John Kennedy makes his "Grand Design" speech.
Jan 14 1963	French President Charles de Gaulle vetoes United Kingdom's application for membership in EEC.
Jun - Dec 1965	"Empty Seat Crisis" within EEC.
Jan 1966	Luxembourg Compromise addresses unanimous voting for EEC.
May 11 1967	President de Gaulle again vetoes Great Britain's entry into the EEC.

1970-1979

Jan 1973	UK, Denmark, and Ireland join the EEC.
1974	European Council established.

1980-1989

Jul 1987	Single European Act signed in Luxembourg.

1990-1999

Oct 1990	German reunification brings former East Germany into the EC.
Feb 1992	Treaty on European Union (Maastricht Treaty) signed. The EC is now referred to as the European Union (EU).
Oct 1997	Treaty of Amsterdam signed, laying the groundwork for upcoming economic and monetary union (EMU).
Jan 1999	EMU goes into effect. The eleven EU member states participating are Austria, Belgium, Finland, France, Germany, Ireland, Italy, Luxembourg, The Netherlands, Portugal, and Spain.

2002

Jan 2002	The "Euro" becomes single currency among participating EU members.

APPENDIX B

Glossary

ACUSE (Action Committee for the United States of Europe): Group founded in 1955 by Jean Monnet to act as a pressure group for closer European integration by bringing together leading personalities of all parties form the Six, plus, in later years, Britain. Dissolved by Monnet in 1975 it had played an important role in the creation of the European Economic Community and strongly opposed the anti-federalist European policies of French President Charles de Gaulle. In the 1985 a successor body, the Action Committee for Europe, was formed but it was far less prominent.

Common Market: This was the name by which the European Community became generally known in the early years of the EEC. The term has since been replaced by the Single Market.

Confederation: Switzerland is Europe's longest standing confederation, involving a combination of local decision-making bodies and central institutions

Congress of Europe: The Congress of Europe, which took place in The Hague in May 1948, led to the foundation of the European Movement in October of the same year. Many of the ideas first aired at the Congress were included in the statute for the Council of Europe a year later.

Council of Europe: The Council of Europe was founded in May 1949 to promote political cooperation between member states and has grown to a membership of 40 countries, plus five who are afforded a 'special guest status'. A Committee of Ministers make the decisions, sometimes on the recommendations of a Parliamentary Assembly, which retains a purely consultative role. A unanimous vote by the Committee of Ministers is necessary for all important decisions. The Council is most concerned with the areas of human rights, education and more recently, constitutional and legislative reform in central and eastern European countries. The Court of Human Rights and the European Commission of Human Rights are both instruments of the Council of Europe.

Council of Ministers: Most of the decisions adopted by the European Union are made by the Council of Ministers, which retains both executive and legislative powers, working closely with the Commission and the European Parliament. Together with the Parliament, the Council authorizes budgetary decisions and is also responsible for negotiations with non-member countries. The Council is composed of a ministerial representative of each member state, who is authorized to commit his/her government to any decisions taken. Presidency of the Council changes every six months. In the Amsterdam Treaty it was agreed that although a few more areas of policy would move from unanimity to qualified majority voting, unanimity is still the rule in crucial areas. Some of the new areas where QMV now applies include: the employment guidelines and incentive measures, social exclusion, equality of men and women, public health, transparency, countering fraud, customs cooperation, treatment of foreign nationals, and research.

Court of Justice: Established in 1951 under the European Coal and Steel Community Treaty, the Court of Justice decides all matters that arise from disputes over Community Treaties or their legislation. Composed of fifteen judges, one from each EU member state, the Court of Justice is the ultimate adjudicator in most matters of EU law. Nine advocates-general assist the judges, their job being to make submissions on cases brought before the court. The powers of the Court of Justice include the authority to impose a fine on any member state which fails to fulfil a treaty obligation.

Empty Chair Crisis: In 1965, Charles de Gaulle instructed all French representatives on the Council of ministers to boycott meetings, and withdrew his country's representative from Brussels. This protest against various operations within the Council, which became known as the Empty Chair Crisis (chaise vide), was ended in January 1966 with the Luxembourg Compromise

European Coal and Steel Community (ECSC): On 9 May 1950, Robert Schuman, who had been aided by Jean Monnet, put forward a proposal to pool French and German coal and steel production under a joint authority, which would be open to other European countries. On 18 April 1951, the European Coal and Steel Community Treaty was signed by Belgium, Germany, France, Italy, Luxembourg and the Netherlands, and the ECSC finally became operational in July 1952. In December 1954, the Britain signed an Association Agreement with the original six signatories. Today, the main role of the ECSC lies in restructuring the Union's steel industry, and providing assistance for miners who have suffered from the decline of the coal industry.

European Council: The president of the European Commission meets regularly with heads of state of member states of the European Community, and these meetings, or summits, are referred to as the European Council. Under the Single European Act, the European Council became an official body within the European Community. The European Council provides a forum for discussion between leaders of the EU member states, while fostering diplomatic relations.

European Defense Community (EDC): The proposal for a European Defense Community was put forward in 1950 by the French government as the Pleven Plan. The EDC was to operate as an army comprising of troops from France, Germany, Italy and the Benelux countries, with a uniform, a flag and a single commander. However, the EDC failed to get the support of the United States, the Britain and even split the French government. Although it was revived as a consideration in 1954, the French National Assembly voted to ensure that it was terminally shelved as a serious option.

European Economic Community (EC): In 1957, the original six signatories ("the Six" of France, Germany, Italy, and the Benelux countries) agreed to the Treaties of Rome, which established the EEC, an open market between member states. Under the Maastricht Treaty, the EEC was renamed the European Union and has expanded to 15 member countries.

European flag: Designed in 1950 and officially approved by the European Commission in 1985, the flag portrays a circle of 12 five-pointed stars on a background of dark blue.

European Movement: The main goal of the European Movement, an inter-country movement that brings together national organizations in 18 countries, is the integration of Europe. Founded in 1948, this umbrella group is composed of groups from 18 countries with the united goal of an integrated Europe. In 1948, the European Movement held a Congress of Europe in The Hague, and since then, it has been influential in many areas of European integration.

European Parliament: The European Parliament began as the Common Assembly, representatives of the member states of the European Coal and Steel Community (ECSC) in 1951. On 1 January, 1958, the Assembly was expanded to include those brought into being by the European Economic Community and Robert Schuman was elected the first president. In March 1962, the Assembly was renamed the European Parliament and later officially changed in the Single European Act. The European Parliament retains budgetary, legislative, statutory and supervisory powers. The first elected Parliament of 1979 to 1984 began the process of consolidating and expanding existing parliamentary powers, while at the same time reforming the institutional structure of the Community. The Parliament also retains substantial powers in relation to the Budget, a fact that has increased tension between the Parliament and the Council arising from budgetary disputes. The Treaty of Amsterdam expanded the authority of the Parliament, extending influence over employment, social policy and the four freedoms. The treaty also cut the different legislative procedures from over 20 to three, along with improving their power over budgetary policy, and set a ceiling of 700 MEPs in the Parliament after enlargement.

European Political Community: The European Political Community grew from an initial proposal in 1950 for a federal army that would be controlled by an elected supranational authority. This suggestion was further examined by the Assembly of the European Coal and Steel Community (ECSC), but it wasn't until March 1953 that a draft Treaty, proposing a European Political Community, was adopted by the then enlarged ECSC Assembly. This EPC was to consist of a two-chamber Parliament, with its administration the responsibility of a European Executive Council. However, the Treaty was eventually abandoned following the vote against the European Defense Community by the French National Assembly in August 1954.

European Union (EU): The European Union brought together all the elements of European Integration such as the European Coal and Steel Community, the European Economic Community and the European Atomic Energy Community. During the early 1980s, steps were taken towards a goal of European Union, which were formalized by the 1986 Single European Act, which outlined the objective of a creation of a European Union in its preamble. The Treaty of European Union was finally signed on 7 February 1992 in Maastricht, and took effect in November of the following year, thus cementing the unification of Europe.

European Free Trade Association (EFTA): The main purpose of the EFTA is to develop economic activity and increase productivity within the member states. Founded in 1960, the original signatories were Austria, Denmark, Norway, Portugal, Sweden, Switzerland and the Britain, known collectively as the Seven. Finland and Iceland joined at later dates. The Association now retains only three member states: Iceland, Norway and Switzerland, as states who subsequently joined the EEC (Britain, Denmark, Portugal) and then the EU (Austria, Finland, Sweden) have withdrawn. The Association Committee has regular contact with the European Parliament.

Fouchet Plan: This denotes the attempt by French President Charles de Gaulle to intergovernmentalize the institutional balance of the European Community and in the process establish a form of cooperation which would secure Europe's independence from the Atlantic Alliance and the United States. Initially the plan was for a union of states to coexist with the existing

Community in a number of new areas, especially in defense, culture and foreign policy. In the end the plan came to nothing but in the early 1960s it did pose a threat to the power and structure of the Community.

General Agreement on Tariffs and Trade (GATT): The GATT convention ties signatory states to the reduction of tariffs and to avoid engaging in unilateral action likely to endanger trade. It defines terms such as dumping and prohibits quantitative restrictions. The signatory states of GATT are together responsible for 90 per cent of world trade. All member states of the Union belong to GATT.

Intergovernmentalism: This term is used to refer to the mechanisms and procedures that have been established in order to facilitate governments working together and cooperating on certain fields while simultaneously retaining their sovereignty. This approach to integration works in opposition to federalism, aiming at keeping supranational institutions to a minimum. The European Free Trade Association and The Organization for Economic Cooperation and Development are examples of organizations that are essentially intergovernmental. Intergovernmentalism is generally considered attractive by espousers of national sovereignty and nationalism.

Maastricht Treaty: The Maastricht Treaty was signed by the member states of the European Communities on 7th February, 1992, and took effect in November of the following year. It contained several amendments to the Treaty of Rome, as well as establishing a Common Foreign and Security Policy and an intergovernmental field of Justice and Home Affairs. Several countries put the treaty to public referenda, with a resounding rejection by the Danish population, and slim majorities in several other EU countries. A second referendum in Denmark secured a majority when the country was given an option to opt-out from stage three of European Monetary Union. Serious difficulties arose on the question of social protocol, with the "social chapter" rejected by the Britain and subsequently removed, resulting in the formation of a Social Community by eleven other signatories, with Britain remaining bound by the social policies of the Single European Act.

Majority Voting: Majority voting refers to a system used by the Council of Ministers as part of the decision-making process. Bigger member states have 'weightier' votes, and therefore have a stronger position within the procedure.

Marshall Plan: In June 1947, US Secretary of State George C. Marshall outlined an offer of aid from the United States to assist in the economic restoration of post-war Europe. The following month, a conference was held in Paris to fine-tune details of a huge program for European recovery. In subsequent years, the United States provided over $13 billion dollars in financial aid to devastated European countries, prompted by fears of the spread of Communism while Europe was unable to defend itself.

NATO: The North Atlantic Treaty Organization was formed in 1949 as a result of deteriorating relations between the United States and the USSR. With the aim of providing collective defense and security it initially involved the United States, Canada and the signatories of the Treaty of Brussels which formed a similar aim between France, Britain and the Benelux countries. Five more joined at the beginning. They were Denmark, Italy, Iceland, Portugal and Norway. By the 1950s Greece, Turkey and West Germany had become members with Spain joining in 1982. However France withdrew from the structure in 1966 and Spain withdrew following a referendum in 1986. Since the end of the Cold War, leading to cuts in defense spending, NATO has had to adjust its role and structure.

Opt-out: This is a facility for member states who choose not to participate in a particular activity of the Union which may be part of a Treaty. It is usually agreed during the negotiations of the Treaty and appears as a protocol to it.

Pan-Europa: As a precursor to the notion of a United Europe, Pan-Europa was suggested as one of a number of so-called 'macronationalisms', which would involve the bringing together of various independent states as one, all-encompassing body. Count Richard Coudenhove-Kalergi proposed the scheme of a Pan-European Union, in his book of the same title.

"Pillars": Under the Maastricht Treaty, the three metaphorical pillars of the European Union are the European Communities, The Common Foreign and Security Policy and the area of Justice and Home Affairs.

Pleven Plan: On 24 October 1950, French Prime Minister Rene Plevin proposed his plan for a European Defense Community to the French National Assembly, who voted in its favor.

Schuman Plan: The Schuman plan took its name from Robert Schuman, the French Foreign Minister who, in collaboration with Jean Monnet, proposed pooling French and German coal and steel production, and placing it under a common Higher authority. Within a year, on 18 April 1951, the European Coal and Steel Community was established, involving France, Germany and the Benelux countries.

Single European Act: The Single European Act was agreed upon in 1986, and entered into force on July 1st of the following year. It laid down the framework for a single European market, and detailed closer cooperation in the fields of environmental, research and technological policies. Through amendments to the Treaties, the Single European Act also ensured further cooperation in the area of foreign policy, under European Political Cooperation.

Single Market: The Single Market comprises all economic activity within the European Community, an internal, common market, governed by a single set of rules. Since January of 1994, the Single Market relates to all of the European Economic Area.

The Six: This term is used to refer to the six original signatories of the Treaty of Paris: France, Germany, Italy, and the Benelux countries (Belgium, the Netherlands, Luxembourg). The Six were the founder members of the European Coal and Steel Community, the European Economic Community and the European Atomic Energy Community.

Sovereignty: Within the European Union, member states retain sovereignty in their ability to opt out of the Union if they choose. However, the Treaty of Rome envisaged independent Higher Authorities that would have sovereign control in the relevant areas. This is effectively what came about, with the institutions of the Union given powers which permit independent action within certain limited spheres. Member states can, in specific situations, be obliged by European law to uphold the responsibilities and obligations their signature entails.

Treaties of Rome : Signed on March 25th 1957 the Treaties establishing the European Economic Community (EEC) and the European Atomic Energy Community (Euratom) were signed by the Six (Belgium, France, Germany, Italy, Luxembourg, Netherlands) in Rome.

Truman Doctrine : The Truman Doctrine comes from an address by US President Harry Truman to the US Congress in 1947 which outlined the US support for resisting the threat of communism throughout the world. It offered support to countries fighting the rise of communism. Its counterpart was the Brezhnev Doctrine of 1968 which similarly proclaimed the right of the Soviet Union to support other Communist states against threats from the west.

United States of Europe : In a speech in Zurich on 19 September 1946 British Prime Minister Winston Churchill made an important speech which introduced the idea of a "United States of Europe". This followed on from his 'iron curtain' address in Fulton, Missouri and made clear his plan that the US of Europe would be a regional organization within the United Nations.

Western European Union (WEU): The WEU was founded in London on the 6 May 1955. It has no independent military capacity of its own, being wholly dependent on forces assigned to it by member states. Its Council is composed of foreign ministers and defense ministers of the 10 members. These are France, Britain, the Benelux countries together with Germany and Italy, Portugal, Spain and Greece. Although the Amsterdam Treaty stated that "the WEU is an integral part of the development of the EU" it stops short of full-merger between the WEU and the EU. The treaty also contained the difficult phraseology for Irish neutrality: "when the Union avails itself of the WEU to elaborate and implement decisions . . . all member states shall be able to participate fully in the tasks in question".

APPENDIX C

"Declaration of Union" [1]

Prime Minister Winston S. Churchill proposal to the British War Cabinet, June 16, 1940

At this most fateful moment in the history of the modern world the Governments of the United Kingdom and the French Republic make this declaration of indissoluble union and unyielding resolution in their common defence of justice and freedom, against subjection to a system which reduces mankind to a life of robots and slaves.

The two Governments declare that France and Great Britain shall no longer be two nations but one Franco-British Union. The constitution of the Union will provide for joint organs of defence, foreign, financial, and economic policies. Every citizen of France will enjoy immediately citizenship of Great Britain, every British subject will become a citizen of France.

Both countries will share responsibility for the repair the devastation of war, wherever it occurs in their territories, and the resources of both shall be equally, and as one, applied to that purpose.

During the war there shall be a single war Cabinet, and all the forces of Britain and France, whether on land, sea, or in the air, will be placed under its direction. It will govern from wherever it best can. The two Parliaments will be formally associated.

The nations of the British Empire are already forming new armies. France will keep her available forces in the field, on the sea, and in the air.

The Union appeals to the United States to fortify the economic resources of the Allies and to bring her powerful material aid to the common cause.

The Union will concentrate its whole energy against the power of the enemy no matter where the battle may be. And thus we shall conquer.

---

[1] Winston S. Churchill, *The Second War World, Vol. II: Their Finest Hour* (New York: Houghton Mifflin Company, 1940), 183-184.

APPENDIX D

"The Tragedy of Europe"[1]

Sir Winston S. Churchill

19 September 1946
Zurich University

I wish to speak to you today about the tragedy of Europe. This noble continent, comprising on the whole the fairest and the most cultivated regions of the earth, enjoying a temperate and equable climate, is the home of all the great parent races of the western world. It is the fountain of Christian faith and Christian ethics. It is the origin of most of the culture, arts, philosophy and science both of ancient and modern times. If Europe were once united in the sharing of its common inheritance, there would be no limit to the happiness, to the prosperity and glory which its three or four hundred million people would enjoy. Yet it is from Europe that have sprung that series of frightful nationalistic quarrels, originated by the Teutonic nations, which we have seen even in this twentieth century and in our own lifetime, wreck the peace and mar the prospects of all mankind.

And what is the plight to which Europe has been reduced? Some of the smaller States have indeed made a good recovery, but over wide areas a vast quivering mass of tormented, hungry, care-worn and bewildered human beings gape at the ruins of their cities and homes, and scan the dark horizons for the approach of some new peril, tyranny or terror. Among the victors there is a babel of jarring voices: among the vanquished the sullen silence of despair. That is all that Europeans, grouped in so many ancient States and nations, that is all that the Germanic Powers have got by tearing each other to pieces and spreading havoc far and wide. Indeed, but for the fact that the great Republic across the Atlantic Ocean has at length realised that the ruin or enslavement of Europe would involve their own fate as well, and has stretched out hands of succor and guidance, the Dark Ages would have returned in all their cruelty and squalor. They may still return.

Yet all the while there is a remedy which, if it were generally and spontaneously adopted, would as if by a miracle transform the whole scene, and would in a few years make all Europe, or the greater part of it, as free and as happy as Switzerland is today. What is this sovereign remedy? It is to recreate the European Family, or as much of it as we can, and provide it with a structure under which it can dwell in peace, in safety and in freedom. We must build a kind of United States of Europe. In this way only will hundreds of millions of toilers be able to regain the simple joys and hopes which make life worth living. The process is simple. All that is needed is the resolve of hundreds of millions of men and women to do right instead of wrong and gain as their reward blessing instead of cursing.

Much work has been done upon this task by the exertions of the Pan-European Union which owes so

---

[1] Winston S. Churchill, *Sinews of Peace, Post-War Speeches* (London: Cassell & Company, Ltd., 1948).

much to Count Coudenhove-Kalergi and which commanded the services of the famous French patriot and statesman, Aristide Briand. There is also that immense body of doctrine and procedure, which was brought into being amid high hopes after the first world war, as the League of Nations. The League of Nations did not fail because of its principles or conceptions. It failed because these principles were deserted by those States who had brought it into being. It failed because the Governments of those days feared to face the facts, and act while time remained. This disaster must not be repeated. There is therefore much knowledge and material with which to build; and also bitter dear-bought experience.

I was very glad to read in the newspaper two days ago that my friend President Truman had expressed his interest and sympathy with this great design. There is no reason why a regional organization of Europe should in any way conflict with the world organization of the United Nations. On the contrary, I believe that the larger synthesis will only survive if it is founded upon coherent natural groupings. There is already a natural grouping in the Western hemisphere. We British have our own Commonwealth of Nations. These do not weaken, on the contrary they strengthen, the world organization. They are in fact its main support. And why should there not be a European group which could give a sense of enlarged patriotism and common citizenship to the distracted peoples of this turbulent and mighty continent and why should it not take its rightful place with the other great groupings in shaping the destinies of men? In order that this should be accomplished there must be an act of faith in which millions of families speaking many languages must consciously take part.

We all know that the two world wars through which we have passed arose out of the vain passion of a newly-united Germany to play the dominating part in the world. In this last struggle crimes and massacres have been committed for which there is no parallel since the invasions of the Mongols in the fourteenth century and no equal at any time in human history. The guilty must be punished. Germany must be deprived of the power to rearm and make another aggressive war. But when all this has been done, as it will be done, as it is being done, there must be an end to retribution. There must be what Mr. Gladstone many years ago called "a blessed act of oblivion." We must all turn our backs upon the horrors of the past. We must look to the future. We cannot afford to drag forward across the years that are to come the hatreds and revenges which have sprung from the injuries of the past. If Europe is to be saved from infinite misery, and indeed from final doom, there must be an act of faith in the European family and an act of oblivion against all the crimes and follies of the past.

Can the free people of Europe rise to the height of these resolves of the soul and instincts of the spirit of man? If they can, the wrongs and injuries which have been inflicted will have been washed away on all sides by the miseries which have been endured. Is there any need for further floods of agony? Is it the only lesson of history that mankind is unteachable? Let there be justice, mercy and freedom. The peoples have only to will it, and all will achieve their hearts' desire.

I am now going to say something that will astonish you. The first step in the re-creation of the European family must be a partnership between France and Germany. In this way only can France recover the moral leadership of Europe. There can be no revival of Europe without a spiritually great France and a spiritually great Germany. The structure of the United States of Europe, if well and truly built, will be such as to make the material strength of a single state less important. Small nations will count as much as large ones and gain their honour by their contribution to the common cause. The ancient states and principalities of Germany, freely joined together for mutual convenience in a federal system, might each take their individual place among the United States of Europe. I shall not try to make a detailed programme for hundreds of millions of people who want to be happy and free, prosperous and safe, who wish to enjoy the four freedoms of which the great President Roosevelt spoke, and live in accordance with the principles embodied in the Atlantic Charter. If this is their wish, they have only to say so, and means can certainly be found, and machinery erected, to carry that wish into full fruition.

But I must give you a warning. Time may be short. At present there is a breathing-space. The cannon have ceased firing. The fighting has stopped; but the dangers have not stopped. If we are to form the United States of Europe or whatever name or form it may take, we must begin now.

In these present days we dwell strangely and precariously under the shield and protection of the atomic bomb. The atomic bomb is still only in the hands of a State and nation which we know will never use it except in the cause of right and freedom. But it may well be that in a few years this awful agency of destruction will be widespread, and the catastrophe following from its use by several warring nations will not only bring to an end to all that we call civilisation, but may possibly disintegrate the globe itself.

I must now sum up the propositions which are before you. Our constant aim must be to build and fortify the strength of U.N.O. Under and within that world concept we must re-create the European family in a regional structure called, it may be, the United States of Europe. The first step is to form a Council of Europe. If at first all the States of Europe are not willing or able to join the Union, we must nevertheless proceed to assemble and combine those who will and those who can. The salvation of the common people of every race and of every land from war or servitude must be established on solid foundations and must be guarded by the readiness of all men and women to die rather than submit to tyranny. In all this urgent work, France and Germany must take the lead together. Great Britain, the British Commonwealth of Nations, mighty America, and I trust Soviet Russia--for then indeed all would be well--must be the friends and sponsors of the new Europe and must champion its right to live and shine.

APPENDIX E

Map of the European Union